One
Hundred
Daffodils

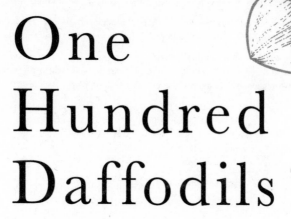

One Hundred Daffodils

*Finding Beauty, Grace, and Meaning
When Things Fall Apart*

Rebecca Winn

GRAND CENTRAL
PUBLISHING

NEW YORK   BOSTON

Grand Central Publishing
Hachette Book Group
1290 Avenue of the Americas, New York, NY 10104
grandcentralpublishing.com
twitter.com/grandcentralpub

First Edition: March 2020

Grand Central Publishing is a division of Hachette Book Group, Inc. The Grand Central Publishing name and logo is a trademark of Hachette Book Group, Inc.

The publisher is not responsible for websites (or their content) that are not owned by the publisher.

The Hachette Speakers Bureau provides a wide range of authors for speaking events. To find out more, go to www.hachettespeakersbureau.com or call (866) 376-6591.

Print book interior design by Thomas Louie.
Daffodil illustration by R. Welairat.

Library of Congress Cataloging-in-Publication Data
Names: Winn, Rebecca, author.
Title: One hundred daffodils : finding beauty, grace, and meaning when things fall apart / Rebecca Winn.
Description: First edition. | New York : Grand Central Publishing, 2020. |
Summary: "A reflection on human resilience and nature's ability to teach, inspire, and heal after an unexpected life upheaval. One Hundred Daffodils is told through the lens of the author's personal experiences with grief and heartbreak on her journey toward self-discovery and empowerment"
—Provided by publisher.
Identifiers: LCCN 2019041836 | ISBN 9781538732700 (hardcover) |
ISBN 9781538732717 (ebook)
Subjects: LCSH: Winn, Rebecca. | Divorced women. | Divorce—Psychological aspects. |
Life change events. | Self-realization in women.
Classification: LCC HQ814 .W625 2020 | DDC 306.89/3—dc23
LC record available at https://lccn.loc.gov/2019041836

ISBNs: 978-1-5387-3270-0 (hardcover), 978-1-5387-3271-7 (ebook)

Printed in the United States of America
LSC-C
10 9 8 7 6 5 4 3 2 1

For Mama

Contents

Contents

Contents

One
Hundred
Daffodils

Prologue

The Spiderweb

There is so much life in the garden. That is why I come. Life that is gentle, self-supporting, and beautiful. Continuous in its cycles, grounded, pure.

On this morning I had come into the garden to escape. The previous night was one of unprecedented upheaval in my marriage. A conflict out of nowhere, or so it seemed, though in retrospect, of course, that's never true. Nevertheless, from my perspective last night, everything appeared to be fine, and then suddenly I was facing a full-on verbal confrontation for which I was totally unprepared.

Sitting safely in the cover of the very early morning mist, I was still in shock. What had just happened? What was going to happen now? I looked out into the gray-lit garden. For a moment, across the path, I noticed a sparkling spiderweb revealed by tiny droplets of moisture deposited by the mist, which was quietly moving on. It was there all along, but from where I was sitting it had been hidden from me. I had not moved, but as everything around me changed minutely with the shifting of the mist, it was revealed to me. A moment later it was gone again, the soft, moist suggestion of secret lines having quickly dried in the light and breeze. But I glimpsed it and felt drawn to it.

Connected by five anchors, breath-like in their fragility, the spider stretches her home boldly across a path from which it could easily be torn. She is quick with her work, as if she knows that forces beyond her control could change her life forever, or end it. Still, with a determination born of instinct, she carefully places the roots of her web and begins to weave her home.

The orb weaver's web is made up of outward stretching lines emanating from a center point around which concentric circles are spun. These coaxial threads are made of a sticky filament to trap the spider's prey. The straight lines are smooth, providing a foundation which allows the spider to move up and down her web without getting bound in it. Parents, spouses, children, jobs, and friends; these anchors provide the foundation around which we spin our ever-tighter lives. The safe lines. The ones we can freely move up and down. They are safe, but fragile. Very fragile. Inevitably, whether from pressure or aggression, one or more of the spider's safe lines could break, leaving the remaining anchors to hold more weight than was entrusted to them. Unmoored now and unstable, the web sags, threatening the future of the spider. If she can re-anchor it in time, her security is ensured for a while, but if more than one anchor is lost, the task ahead will be daunting.

I am not sure how many of my safe lines snapped last night, but I feel a great urgency to try to reattach what I can. To try to preserve some semblance of safety for my home and family.

I tried to walk up to the spiderweb, searching for a clearer view, but found, as I approached, I couldn't see it at all. It seemed to disappear into the shadows. I glanced around to see if I was obscuring my own light. Through the shifting morning mist, sometimes when I looked at the sunrays, I saw lines of light. Sometimes they were lines of shadow. The mist tumbled by through light, through shadow, and then it was gone. Standing just above the spot where I was sure her web had been, I was puzzled that I could not find it at all from this close position. Clarity came from a distance. I stepped back and it appeared. I stepped forward and it vanished. As I changed my perspective, the web appeared, then disappeared, then appeared again. Somehow, knowing it was there didn't help me find it at all. I had to move away to regain the perspective I had lost. I needed to step back to understand what happened last night. I needed to gain perspective.

As I tried to center on this, my thoughts fell back to a few moments before, when I had wondered if I was obscuring my own light. In that moment, this question of simple physics began to spread wider and became abstract. I *was* obscuring my own light. I had been for years. I had done it thinking that I was doing what was best for my family, but in making the choice over and over again to hide my light, I had reduced myself to someone who was fearful and dependent. Someone who had traded independence for security provided by another to whom I had freely, though foolishly, given all my power. In doing what I thought would make me safe, I had in fact made myself vulnerable. Deeply, frighteningly vulnerable. My marriage was in danger, and I realized in a moment of crystal clarity that I needed to find out who I was, why this was happening, and what, if anything, I could do to save it.

The mist was moving on, and the sun peeked over the horizon behind me. As it rose, a long shadow stretched out before me. My Shadow. And I knew I had to walk into it.

Form and Formlessness

It is nice to be able to sit by running water. I feel far away. A floating sensation almost like an out-of-body experience I have felt ever since the conflict with my husband the other night. Maybe I'm still in shock. There is an element to this feeling of being only semiconscious of the present. Like being in deep thought on a long road trip, and suddenly realizing you've gone a hundred miles without noticing anything you've driven past. My attention is about 10 percent in the present while the remaining 90 percent is recycling scattered bits of what happened the other night, trying to piece them together, but nothing seems to fit.

The thick morning mist is beginning to envelop me, and the cover it provides is comforting. As the sunlight finds its way through the leaves, it gives streaked, dappled form to the shapeless fog, as if its rays are trying to contain the mist—give it some kind of parameters. But it shifts and rolls with the slightest breeze, refusing to be contained in any way. So it is with my thoughts...my life. Rolling, tumbling, reaching out like a modern dancer trying to grab on to an invisible...something, some fragment of understanding, only to have it disappear before I can get hold. If the light falls on me, will it give me form? Would I even want it to if it could? Here in this place of solitude and contemplation, I can be in the formlessness where I hope understanding resides, though I can't seem to find it. Veiled in the soft mist, I can think. But thinking isn't what I need right now. What I need is to feel. But I can't feel anything. I'm numb. I think I want to be in the feelings, immersed in them, consumed by them, guided by them. But there I go again, thinking.

I'm grateful for the fog. It makes me invisible.

I can feel the mist in my nostrils as I inhale. It's cool and damp and more tactile than air usually is. I take in the formlessness. I breathe it in. I let the formlessness expand in my lungs and fill me up; then I exhale and close my eyes. I envision the formlessness as it enters me, erasing all thoughts, all emotions, all sensation, making them invisible, like me. I visualize the formlessness. It moves from my lungs, deep into my core, through organs and body systems. It radiates out to my smallest extremities, wiping away the data, the attachments, the stories held within. I envision the formlessness being pulled around me, drawing power and momentum from the whole forest toward me, down through my head, in with my breath, seeping into every pore, until I do not exist at all. The formlessness fills me. It becomes me. It cracks me open to the void. Open, empty, sponged out. In the void, I am formless. In the void, there is no I am. There is no I. There is no...

A gust shifts the air. A streak of light breaks through. It's early morning, but I'm drained and can't resist, even though I want to stay here alone in the formlessness, invisible. Indifferent to my preferences, the light sits beside me, a wordless, well-meaning friend. We sit in silence for a while; then she whispers to me through the mist.

"Light and shadow are what we're made of. Together they create form. Both are worthy. Both are needed. Both are welcome."

I am Light. I am Shadow.

So is he.

Chapter 1

Decomposition

Living in Sleeping Beauty's Castle

PART ONE

From the moment I moved into this house, I began to sequester. Partially by choice, and partially because our family moved north a few miles and crossed an emotional boundary that most people who lived in my old neighborhood considered too far to easily drive for a visit. That was a big change for me because our last house had been one block behind a popular Starbucks, so every few days, one friend or another would call and say, "Hey, I'm at the Starbucks and thought I'd drop by. You want anything?" I loved the spontaneity and the frequent surprise company, never knowing who might call or stop in for a visit.

The neighborhood where I was born is a small town within a big city, both literally and as a lived experience. A small, established, close-knit community in the center of Dallas, Texas, the Park Cities is made up of two small towns: Highland Park and University Park. Each town has its own mayor and its own city council, and they share an independent school district. Just like many small towns, there are people whose families have lived in the Park Cities for three or four generations, and they have no interest whatsoever in that, or anything else, changing. I myself am third generation. My son is fourth. Neighbors know each other, have block parties, and bring food when someone dies. A simple trip to the grocery store for milk and eggs can take more than an hour, depending on how much time is spent chatting with friends while there.

But as soon as I moved north of Interstate 635, people suddenly acted like they needed to update their passports just to come see me. Even my good friends. Even though it took only seven minutes on the North Tollway to get to my new house from my old neighborhood, and even though it could take up to twenty minutes to get across the old neighborhood to my house because I lived on the far eastern edge. But somehow the trek north was daunting enough to be a deal breaker for most people, most of the time.

At first it really hurt my feelings. A lot. In fact, it really hurt my feelings a lot for a long time. But then, I began to realize that my choice of neighborhood was no accident. I told myself, and those who asked, that I chose this house in this neighborhood because the property on which the house sat was a blank slate and a thrilling near half acre. A lot that size would have cost well into seven or even eight figures in the Park Cities, if half-acre lots even existed there, which mostly they do not. But something else was at work when I chose this house. Something deeper and much more important than my excitement about having a large garden to create from scratch.

The truth was, my marriage had continued to deteriorate since that first explosive night, and when I started looking for this house, I could tell at an unspoken level that Daniel didn't really want to buy another house together. So he just let me do the research and all the legwork. When I found this house, he agreed to it, though he never really seemed very interested. We had been married almost twenty-four years and had bought quite a few houses together. We always bought fixer-uppers because we both enjoyed the process of restoring old homes. But this time, he was very hands-off. So I took the reins, found the house, oversaw the purchase, and managed the remodeling myself, all the while knowing we had big problems.

I had wanted to build a small wall around the front to create a courtyard entry, but with all the other work the house needed, we decided that little detail was too expensive, so when it was time to do the landscaping, I achieved the desired courtyard effect by encircling the front entry with a new variety of landscape roses that no one knew much about at the time, called Knockout roses. The label said they would grow to be three to four feet tall and equally wide, which would make a perfect green enclosure for the front patio. Even better than a wall, I decided, because the enclosure would be roses. In the years to come, Knockout roses would make horticultural history and become the most glorious and ubiquitous of landscape roses, but that's another story. In this story, within a year of moving into this house, my husband told me he wanted a divorce, and shortly thereafter, he moved out.

The roses around my house were growing fast. By the end of the second year, they were already over five feet tall, and I had begun to joke that I lived in Sleeping Beauty's castle. There were roses all the way around the courtyard and across the entire front of the house, turning the corner at the property's edge, then continuing down the side of my lot to the street, and across the front at the curb. It was a lot of roses, but as I always say, "More, by definition, is more," because where flowers are concerned, I don't believe in too much of a good thing.

Almost twice as high and wide now as they were supposed to be at full maturity, the roses had grown together and it was impossible to see where one rosebush ended and the next began. It was a veritable Great Wall of Roses that had long since obscured the window boxes on the front of the house, and now they were even beginning to cover the windows. I told myself that I felt safer living alone in the house surrounded by my thorny guardians.

Whenever my husband would come over to collect his mail or get more clothes, he would comment that he was surprised I had let everything get so "overgrown." I basically ignored him, chalking his comments up to yet another criticism that no longer mattered to me, and besides, I thought the roses were amazing. Yes, they had probably gotten too big for the location, and yes, I could have trimmed them, but they were massive *rose*bushes, and they were beautiful. Big, yes. Too big, maybe. But beautiful. And frankly, the more he would insinuate that I was doing it wrong by letting them get "overgrown," the less likely I was to trim them. Passive-aggressive? Yep. On both our parts. But communication had always been our greatest failing.

At the same time, I felt an increasing need to further enclose my property, so I added a line of six-foot-tall, full-to-the-ground cherry laurels around the front perimeter. I wasn't thinking too much about why I felt the need to do this, but when my neighbors across the street commented that they could never tell if I was home because of my "privacy landscaping," I realized for the first time what I was doing. I was pulling in. I had planted a protective fortification around myself that was designed to keep everyone out because I wanted and needed to be alone. I wanted and needed time to figure out who I was, where my life had derailed, and what I was going to do next. The only way that felt safe was within the confines of this beautiful floral fortress. Like Sleeping Beauty, I had surrounded myself with a forest of thorns while my heart and psyche slept in a cocoon of process as I tried to make sense of my life.

Carl Jung defined our Shadow as those aspects within us we have subconsciously disowned. These aspects are personal qualities of which we are unaware, though the joke among my more conscious friends is that everyone else is acutely aware of our Shadow aspects, particularly our close friends and intimate partners. Ours, but not their own, of course, because this is the work we each must do. I believe it is our souls' work to uncover our disowned aspects, both the glorious and the hideous. And then we must find a way to embrace and unify all aspects of ourselves, because this is the place where understanding, forgiveness, and true peace reside. Or so I hear. I personally have no direct experience of anything so profound, though I do aspire to it. This personal work is essential for us to grow, heal, and expand our consciousness, for the good of ourselves and each other. If we do not, we shall go on hurting others, hurting ourselves, allowing others to hurt us, and hurting the earth. I knew at an intuitive level that I had to enter into the darkness of this work. To do that, I needed to turn inward. So, in moments of grace, both great and small, my garden wrapped itself around me in a protective embrace as I embarked on this journey of self-discovery.

During this time, my son, Alexander, with whom I am very close, had been away at the University of Southern California, pursuing his dream of becoming a filmmaker. I was thrilled for him to have been accepted into the most prestigious film school in the world, but it was far away, and I missed him terribly. In an effort to try to stay connected to the life I knew, I had been back to visit friends in my old neighborhood many times, but in the first couple of years, only three of my closest friends had ever come to see me at my new house. For a while, after my husband moved out, I spent all my time just getting my head around coming home to an empty house and feeling into this new experience. My marriage was ending. My husband was gone, and my friends were drifting away as well.

Then one day, as the shifting reality of both my marriage and my friendships became clearer, I had an epiphany. I realized that nearly all of the people I spent time with were either the daughters of my mother's friends, the wives of my husband's friends, or the mothers of my son's friends, some of whom I loved dearly. But how many of my friends had I actually chosen? And of those people I thought of as my friends, how many would I choose today?

Up until this point, everything felt as if it was happening *to* me—the separation in my marriage, the distance from my son, the lack of connection with my friends and their apparent indifference toward the preservation of our friendships. But what if, rather than continuing to make herculean efforts to preserve all these old connections, I decided to do a fruit basket turnover with all my relationships? What if I could actually choose, for once, the people with whom I wanted to spend my time? What would that even feel like? I had never done it before. Ever since my family moved to Europe when I was in first grade, causing me to change not only schools but countries every few years, I was always the new girl, never in one place long enough to forge lasting friendships, always feeling alone and isolated, always waiting to be chosen by someone who might notice me and reach out to this shy, foreign little girl and make her feel welcome and wanted. I never felt I had the time, the power, or even the right to choose my friends. I was always waiting to be chosen.

And here was that same shy, wounded little girl, sitting now on her sofa decades later, feeling yet again like the unchosen one. But what if I did something different this time? If I could actually choose my friends, what would they be like? Who would I choose to spend my time with if I could pick anyone out of the great well of potential people in the world?

I hardly knew where to begin.

Desperately
Seeking Self

Have you ever used an old-fashioned pressure cooker? You can hardly find them to buy anymore. They've been replaced by safer, less intimidating, digital Instant Pots. But if you've ever seen a real pressure cooker in action, you know they are pretty memorable. I was afraid of them when I was a little girl, probably because my mother would always have my sister and me stand across the room when she was cooking with one. Mama's pressure cooker was a large pot—probably eight to ten quarts—with a metal lid that somehow magically bent to fit inside the rim of the pot. It had a big, black, industrial latch she pushed down to lock the lid snugly into place. When she turned on the heat, pressure built up inside the tightly sealed pot, thus cooking the food much faster. There was a little relief valve

21

on the lid of the pot with a weighted, free-floating metal pressure regulator that jiggled as the pressure rose inside, allowing a small, continuous amount of steam to release from the pot, to keep it from exploding. Yes, actually exploding. The greater the pressure inside the pot, the more the pressure regulator jiggled, sometimes ramping up to a rapid, loud clatter. You were never supposed to lift the pressure regulator off the steam vent or touch it at all, as accidental or intentional removal would allow hot steam to shoot out of the vent like an oil-rig blowout, and could be very dangerous.

The weeks between when Daniel told me he wanted a divorce and when he moved out, I felt like Mama's pressure cooker. Pressure had been building up inside me for years without my acknowledgment, but now, with relief in sight, my little pressure regulator had passed jiggling and was starting to clatter. Dan and I had agreed he would stay in the house until our son came home for spring break, and we would tell him together about our decision to separate. We planned to tell him the day after he got home, but Daniel's father died unexpectedly in a car accident that day. In an instant, all other plans were pushed aside, and we spent the week making arrangements and having his funeral. In the flurry and chaos, we ended up not telling Alex about our decision to separate until the day before he was going back to college. In hindsight, that was terribly unfair to him, but we were all so shocked and surprised by Grandpa's death, the news of our separation was all but forgotten until the very last minute before he left.

As fate would have it, though, the timing was a blessing in a way. I was glad we never had to tell Dan's father we were splitting up. He would not have taken it well. After having five sons that included two sets of twins, both he and Dan's mother were thrilled when I came into the family and could be the daughter they had always wanted. His mother had passed away several years before, so Grandpa was the last remaining member of the older generation in either of our families. A dynamic, bombastic retired attorney, Grandpa would not only have objected to our decision, I am reasonably sure he would have tried to assert some kind of authority to stop it, which would not have been helpful. Terrible though Grandpa's sudden death was, it made two bad situations a little better for Daniel, because we never had to tell his dad, and instead of having to rent a place, he just moved into his parents' house, making it easier both to relocate and to deal with estate issues.

Somewhere along the line, a little over halfway into our marriage, Dan had gotten angry at me. Or more accurately, Dan had gotten angry. I'm not sure it was really at me. At least not at first. Just that fact alone was alarming and hard to grasp because he had always been such a convivial, easygoing guy. But there were problems at work. Specifically, a nightmare client who had already chewed through seven lawyers on the same case before she came to Dan, and who proceeded to make his life a living hell for a few years.

If we had started going to couple's therapy at that time, things might have turned out differently. But we didn't, and it didn't. Instead, I began to withdraw while he got more angry, and the safest place for him to express that was at me. Since I knew what was going on in his life, I tried not to take it personally. I thought (and still think) that was the wise and loving thing to do, at least at first. What was not wise or loving (at least to myself) was that I never set any kind of boundary on the behavior. That's on me. I guess I thought it would pass when he was able to get out from under that client. But as months turned into years, his frustration became stronger, and my ability to shake it off grew weaker, so I began to absorb the blame that was being cast my way. In time, his criticism became less localized and more all-encompassing. It had become a habit. I figured out far too late that in marriage, just as with gardens, a good plan is important, but over time, incremental maintenance is key.

As with many things in my life, I should have seen it coming when Daniel told me he wanted a divorce, but I didn't. I always described him as the most honorable person I had ever met, and loyal to a fault. That "loyal to a fault" part showed up as a lifelong pattern of staying in friendships and professional relationships that were not healthy or equal to him. It was easy to see this frustrating flaw in him, but only now do I realize it was a pattern we shared. When Daniel was still practicing law, he had a secretary for years who was an active heroin addict. Uncertain of how to help and not wanting to interfere, he just kept her on as if nothing was wrong until the day she died of an overdose. Based on this and other less dramatic but equally obvious instances, it truly never occurred to me he would ever ask me for a divorce. So when he did, I was completely caught off guard. To be honest, a part of me was tremendously relieved. I wanted out, but by then I was so depressed, emotionally damaged, and crushingly disempowered, I don't think I ever could have mustered the courage to leave.

Another part of me, a much bigger part, was terrified. I had worked as a fashion model when I was younger and taught at a couple of modeling and finishing schools while I was in college and for several years after graduation. I had also sold real estate early in our marriage. But I am a caregiver at heart, so when our son was born, there was nowhere I wanted to be but with him. I was incredibly lucky to be able to spend his childhood years as a stay-at-home mother, for which I was so grateful, and I loved every minute of it.

When Alexander reached fourth grade, my husband started working for a nonprofit. To help out financially, I took my love of gardening and my degree in fine art and started designing landscapes for other people. I had no formal training in garden design, and didn't even know how to draw to scale at the time, but having won scores of floral design awards and over three hundred horticulture awards in garden club flower shows, I had developed a reputation for being a gardening expert (which was probably not altogether true at the time, at least not at a professional level). Nevertheless, because of numerous requests from friends to help them with their gardens, one day I declared myself a landscape designer, and Whimsical Gardens was born. But it had never generated a great deal of income. In fact, I had never fully supported myself financially—not even close—

and the prospect of starting now, when I was pushing fifty, was scary to the point of being paralyzing.

Our discussions about separating mostly took place on our back patio at night. I don't remember how many there were, but there were quite a few. I just remember the first one, and the last one. I remember the first one because of the obvious shock. I remember the last one because of a much less obvious shock. I was expressing my fear of being able to support myself, and Dan said, "You know, I can't even imagine how high you could fly without my wet blanket." You could have knocked me over with a pansy. When Dan and I were dating and first married, I used to say he believed in me more than I believed in myself. But that guy seemed to have long since caught another boat going a different direction. This guy had been criticizing everything I did for years now. I could barely believe what I was hearing. But given how the last few years had played out, these words, from a flicker of the man I had married, in a rare moment of self-awareness, were extremely powerful.

After our son went back to school, we both knew that Daniel would be moving out at some point, but we had not discussed any specifics around timing. A couple of weeks later, I had enrolled in a weekend workshop out of town. When I returned that Sunday afternoon, Dan was gone. No notice, no word, no goodbye, no note, no nothing. He was just gone. On the day before our twenty-fifth wedding anniversary, no less. It was the strangest, most jarring experience. It made me so angry that even given our very civil agreement to separate, when he moved out, he had somehow managed to make me feel "left," deserted, abandoned. It felt so rude. So inconsiderate. Almost aggressive. So not the way I would have done it. Turns out, he thought it would be easier, more considerate. We were so far off the same page by then, we weren't even in the same library.

After I got over the stabbing, archaic abandonment trigger that Dan's unscheduled and unannounced exit caused, though, I was like a pressure cooker after the heat has been turned off. My internal pressure regulator slowed from a clatter to a jiggle to a slow rocking as my emotional steam eased with an audible sigh. It didn't evaporate, but it dialed way down. Without the constant stress of living with someone for whom I could do nothing right, every day that I awoke in my house alone, every day I drove up to my house and his car was gone, every day as I walked through my house and the tension and angry energy was absent, I breathed more easily, and a great weight began to lift from my heart. I journaled daily. I wrote about my feelings, I wrote about my garden, I wrote about my fears, I wrote about my dreams. Sometimes I wrote all day for days on end. I spent a lot of time reading, too. Reading about relationships, reading about codependency (man...those were eye-opening), reading about adverse childhood experiences, about spirituality, about self-help. I have a pretty serious learning difference that makes reading hard for me. I read very slowly, and it is in no way a pleasurable experience, but I was reading multiple books at a time for hours every day, while also going to therapy and as many healing workshops as I could afford. I believed all my suffering was Daniel's fault. He believed absolutely everything was my fault. It was early in my journey to understanding, but that disparity was so big and so clear, I was sure it was a clue worth exploring. We couldn't both be right. But we probably weren't both wrong either. So what was the truth?

It was in these hours, days, weeks, and months of intensive study, self-analysis, and process writing that I began to dial in so closely to my garden. It was a beautiful garden, floriferous, fragrant, and inviting. I didn't understand this at the time, but being in the garden was grounding for me. Feeling my feet on the earth, breathing floral scented air, noticing line, form, color, and condition changing minutely each time I went out, all lifted me from my emotional torment and brought me back to the present moment in connection with the garden. I spent as much time as I could there, or sitting on my covered back porch, where I could still be outside, no matter if it was scalding hot, pouring rain, sleeting, or even snowing. I filled up spiral notebook after spiral notebook with my thoughts, feelings, and musings. I did self-help exercises, recorded dreams, and wrote letters I never intended to send. I spent so much time alone trying to understand my life that I would not see or speak to anyone sometimes for days or even a week at a time. I was surrounded and protected by my rose fortress, and I had a job to do. It wasn't the job Dan wanted me to get, but it was the job my soul demanded.

I had been a student of spiritual psychology and New Thought for several years and started going to three sacred services every Sunday morning. I went to two different churches at nine and at eleven thirty and then to the Dallas Meditation Center on Sunday evenings to study with Brother ChiSing Eng, who had a master of divinity in Christian theology from Baylor University and was an ordained disciple of Thich Nhat Hanh, the world-famous Zen master. It was full-on, full-time, broad-spectrum immersion in analysis, spiritual development, and personal growth.

I joined the choir at both my churches because I knew part of my task was to find my voice. Not my singing voice, but my authentic voice. I hoped singing might be the gateway to my true voice, which had been hushed decades ago, then silenced in recent years. I enjoyed singing, and had a decent choir voice but always said I was not a soloist because my voice was not strong enough. However, the reality was, my voice was very strong when I was singing in a choir. It got weak when I tried to sing alone. This was not a vocal problem. This was something else, and it felt like a piece to the same puzzle. Who am I apart from my role as a wife and a mother? Do I have any value outside of those roles? What am I going to do with my life? Where do I belong? What is my purpose? Do I even have a purpose? Is there such a thing as a pointless person? Do I matter at all? I had no clue, but I was determined to find out.

When I embarked on this journey of self-discovery, I didn't know how long it would take, how difficult it would be, or what twists and turns were in store for me. One thing was clear, though. The life I knew was dissolving, and the question was no longer whether or not I could stop it. I didn't want to stop it. I wanted to understand it. This illusion in which I had been living—this script I had been acting out—was never a script of my creation or even my choosing, at least not consciously.

I had been raised to be a certain kind of girl, and I had dutifully followed the path laid out before me. Brought up in a very sheltered, conservative, traditional home, I was spoon-fed the expected "dream" my whole life. A husband, a home, children, helping my husband build his career. The concept of my own career was not only never discussed, it was actively looked down upon. Ladies do not compete with their husbands. I was actually told not to learn to balance my checkbook because that would be my husband's responsibility. I had never before questioned my prescribed role. I didn't think of it as disempowering. It was just the way it was. I adored my mother. I *wanted* to be like her. There was no part of me that wanted to disrespect her guidelines for life. It never occurred to me that I had alternatives. My world was small, but it was lovely. At least on the outside.

Yet now, faced with the death of that illusion, I had an opportunity, a second chance. I was literally *dis*-illusioned from a false dream that had never been my own in the first place, and this time, I was choosing the road far less traveled by the women of my world. I didn't want to immediately find another man. I wanted to find myself. So I waded out into the vast sea of uncertainty. Into the infinite unknown. I was sure I was out there somewhere.

Living in Sleeping Beauty's Castle

PART TWO

The concept of choosing the people with whom I would associate was so foreign to me that it took me a good while to get comfortable with it. It took me no time, however, to stop trying to force the maintenance of past relationships with people who were not reciprocating. As soon as I became conscious of the fact that my whole life, I had waited to be chosen and had settled for relationships that were less than ideal because of it, I was pretty much finished with that. I had extricated myself from destructive relationships in the past, but not without a great deal of drama (mostly internal drama of my own making), even more heartache, and often not until the degree to which they were destructive to me had become so extreme, I was completely miserable. And once, just out of college, I was in real physical danger when an abusive boyfriend slammed me up against a wall and threatened to rape me when I told him I wanted to break up. Now, with this new, clearer perspective, as I looked back over my past relationships, I realized that the unhealthy ones far outnumbered the loving ones. Indeed, it was safe to say the close, truly loving, supportive relationships throughout my life could have been counted on one hand, with room to spare. I was genuinely surprised to discover that my whole life I had been drawn to diminishing, abusive relationships like a moth to the fires of Mount Doom.

In one such incident, when I was in my early thirties, I reached a breaking point with a woman I considered at the time to be my closest friend, whom I will call Julia. Julia and I spent so much time together, people would frequently ask if we were sisters, and commented on how much we looked like each other. We thought this was hilarious because she was barely five feet tall, with olive skin, dark eyes, and black hair, whereas I was almost five feet nine, with blue eyes, very fair skin, and auburn hair. In other words, we looked *nothing* like each other, but apparently, we had picked up mannerisms and speech patterns that made us resemble one another, at least energetically.

For some time, I had had a vague sense that Julia was a much better friend to me when I was struggling than she was when I was experiencing success or good fortune. The truth is, when anything good happened to me, she would damn by faint praise at best and was more often downright caustic. But she was so kind, helpful, and supportive when things went wrong, I focused on those times and tried to forget the flip side. Julia had always been very competitive within the friendship, especially where our husbands were concerned, but at the time I didn't have the emotional or relational tools to even identify that behavior, let alone set boundaries to stop it. Finally, after eleven years of talking on the phone every day and going almost everywhere together, I realized her competitive nature had reached an all-time low when she used it against my three-year-old son. I was so devastated when I realized what she had done that I simply cut off all communication with her without a word, which was not that easy to do before caller ID. But when I was done, I was done.

Since we spent so much time together over so many years, people naturally began asking me where she was when I showed up places without her. One day, I ran into a friend of Julia's I barely knew, who asked me about her absence. When I replied that I was no longer associating with her, the woman snorted and said, "Well, none of us could ever understand why you were friends with her anyway. She was always so mean to you."

I was absolutely dumbstruck. I had always felt in my heart that Julia said cruel things to me, and diminished me in front of others, but no matter how hurtful the things she said and did were, I had dismissed them, thinking I was being too sensitive or that I had somehow misunderstood. I so desperately wanted to believe I was making a bigger deal of it than it was, it truly never occurred to me that others might have noticed and felt the same way about her behavior. I loved her and was in deep denial about the reality of how she treated me. I wanted to believe that she loved me, too. And maybe she did in her way. But her jealousy and competitiveness within the friendship were deeply dysfunctional, and as long as I was in it, I was colluding in my own abuse. As shocking, painful, and embarrassing as this woman's assessment of my friendship with Julia was, it was also validating. A confirmation of my sense that this was not how friends should treat each other, and an early signal that my willingness to suffer such shabby treatment, though extensive, was not without limits. Small steps...

Fast forward eighteen years. Okay, slow forward. After all, it was eighteen years later. Maybe I'm not a quick study, but I do eventually learn. Committed and cautiously excited, I initiated the daring adventure of picking my friends by making a New Life friend sheet, which consisted of a list of all the qualities I could think of that I admired in people. Qualities that I would like to spend more time around, such as having more than a passing interest in psychology and personal growth, being environmentally conscious, having heart-centered ambition, and being spiritually aligned. People who were trying to live a larger, more expansive life while also having a positive impact on humanity and the earth. I then made a list of people I currently knew, however peripherally, who seemed to possess these qualities, and I set about cultivating those relationships. I also opened myself emotionally and energetically to meeting new people who were in possession of the qualities I had listed on my New Life friend sheet.

One day, without notice of the correlation, I trimmed my rosebushes for the first time since they had been planted. They had now reached a whopping seven feet tall. Much like Dan's surprise assessment of my potential, at this point, part of me was just curious how big these roses would get if left to their own devices. How "high they could fly." I trimmed them judiciously because at some level, their great size and thorny branches still made me feel safe, but I took them back about twelve to eighteen inches. This was almost an exercise in "why bother" because no one but me would even notice they were any shorter, since they still towered over most people. It was a small change, but to my eye it felt a little more open, while at six feet high, they still made a comfortingly vicious and impenetrable fortress around my home and my healing heart.

By Christmas the following year, I had connected with a nice new group of friends, and decided to have a party for my birthday between Christmas and New Year's Eve. Just before the party, I transplanted some hollies that had grown to be about seven feet tall and were completely blocking the front windows outside my studio. Suddenly, new light poured into the space where I create. I felt that on every level.

An interesting thing happens when one chooses one's own associations. The assessment of whether they are supportive and enriching is easier to see. When one is always waiting to be chosen, the chooser has all the power, while the choosee, desperate to hang on to whatever time and attention the chooser is willing to dole out, feels grateful for whatever pittance she receives. This makes it virtually impossible to determine whether or not you are actually safe and happy in the relationship, because you are so busy just trying to hang on to it. As I began to step into the power of choosing my relationships, it also became easier to release those that proved to be unhealthy, dysfunctional, or nonreciprocal. This was a high step for me.

A few months after I had trimmed my roses to about six feet tall around the front of my house, I noticed an interesting shift. They had begun to feel crowded and made me feel a little closed in. They looked a bit harsh to me now. The thorns seemed more prominent than the flowers. My self-imposed solitary confinement was lifting for the moment. I felt that in my heart, and I noticed it in my garden. As I walked through the rose walls around my house, I had an urge to open up the space and let in more light. Even as I still felt the sadness and heartache of my separation and trepidation about my future, my world was beginning to open up, and my need to sequester was falling away. It was time to welcome both the light and the Light back into my home and my heart.

Déjà Vu All Over Again

The first time I sought professional counseling services was when I decided to "divorce" Julia. I was thirty-three years old. At that time, personal failures such as "needing a shrink" were spoken of only in hushed tones in polite society. And by Woody Allen on screen, but he was no role model. Going into therapy conjured frightening images of "insane asylums" and Jane Eyre. I knew of only a couple of people who had ever been in therapy, and they weren't just trying to sort out their lives; they were seriously mentally ill. Furthermore, one of them was Dan's oldest brother, who had suffered what used to be called a nervous breakdown during his freshman year at Brown University. He was ultimately diagnosed with schizophrenia and spent the rest of his life in and out of full-time care. But not before the psychiatrists had compounded the family trauma by blaming his mother for his mental illness in the grossly misguided Freudian fashion of the time.

Even in the face of the failure of therapy in my limited experience, I was in enough pain that I was still willing to seek help. But with a toddler at home, I didn't have a lot of time, and we didn't have a lot of money to throw at something that was simultaneously considered counterproductive and a luxury—a waste of both time and money. I quietly asked around, and got a couple of recommendations that were too expensive to justify. Then one day some friends at the church where Dan and I married mentioned that the ministers were also licensed counselors and offered marriage counseling to members for free. I figured that was close enough, and the price was right, so I took the first appointment they had open.

Reverend Beverly was a serious but accessible looking woman, probably in her midfifties. As soon as I sat down, I tearfully blurted out a string of mean, critical, backstabbing things Julia, my closest friend of the last eleven years, had done and said to me. I told her how a part of me wanted to cut Julia out of my life altogether, but another part was deeply conflicted about doing it. I finally drew a breath after about half an hour, paused, and said, "I guess I just need someone to tell me it's okay for me to do this."

"All right," she replied matter-of-factly, "it's okay for you to do this."

Then after a beat she said, "Now, let's talk about why it has taken you eleven years to do it."

Honestly, I was kind of taken aback. I didn't really know what to expect from counseling, but it sure wasn't this. I wanted her to tell me how right and justified I was. How bad and wrong Julia was. I wanted her to sympathize with me and validate my victimhood. I wanted her to tell me she understood my struggle about divorcing my best friend, empathize with my desperate worry over whether Julia would be okay without me, identify with my immersion in the friendship. Instead, the thing I was having so much trouble with—ditching Julia—was a no-thing for Rev. Bev. After her almost flippant "yeah—do that" reaction, she wanted to dig straight into me and my choices. About what was driving me to stay in such an unhealthy friendship for so long. Almost as if she was looking for what was wrong with *me*. Uh...okay. This isn't where I thought we would go, but I guess I'm open.

The first few weeks, I found counseling frustrating. I hashed and rehashed all the ways in which Julia had betrayed me and treated me horribly. Rev. Bev listened and acknowledged me, but never seemed to offer any answers, explanations, or solutions. She just kept asking me questions. I don't remember most of the questions she asked, but I do remember, as my aggravation built, thinking, "If I knew the answer to that, I wouldn't need you!" Then one day, as I was elaborating on my list of Julia's offenses yet again, she asked, "Who is Julia to you?" At first, I didn't understand the question. Julia was Julia. Who else would she be? She asked again, "Who is Julia to you?" I think I just stared at her, toying with the idea that she might not be too bright, clearly had not been listening to me for the last six weeks, and definitely didn't "get it."

When the session was over, I huffed out of the building, into a beautiful spring day, frustrated and super annoyed, thinking, "Well, you get what you pay for." Then, as I walked across the parking lot to my car, I was suddenly broadsided by a searing flash of molten realization. She was Bon Bon! Oh my God... *Julia was Bon Bon!*

I turned and ran back into the building, bolted up the stairs, and burst into Rev. Bev's office. "She's my grandmother!" I exclaimed, and I burst into tears.

"Sit down," she said.

I stayed another two hours, sobbing as I explained the lifetime of verbal and emotional abuse I had suffered at the hands of Bon Bon, my paternal grandmother.

That day I stepped into another dimension. A parallel reality of my own life that had existed all along, side by side with the one I knew. The first portal to healing had just been opened as if by Dr. Strange. And strange it was. For the next two and a half decades, I would be made increasingly aware that inhabiting a body and having a mind does not necessarily mean you know anything about either of those two things. I would learn in time that there were scores of things I believed I understood about my life, my intimate relationships, each of the people with whom I associated, and the circumstances around my life's events, only to find out later how wrong I was. My body would house experiences and emotions my mind could not handle or process, and when my vessel became overloaded with sublimated experiences and emotions, they would morph and manifest as bizarre ailments, infirmities, and afflictions. As my sister once said, "You never get anything normal." It was practically true. Because basically every weird affliction that plagued my body had begun as an emotional wound. The symptoms were not imagined. They were real, visible, diagnosable events in my body. But they were all psychosomatic in origin.

Over the years, I brought many painful relationships and experiences into therapy. Each one looked unique at first, but in time, as we dialed into the deeper nuances of the person, series of behaviors, or events, it always came back to Bon Bon. Even as I matured and grew more and more conscious of the wounds that drove so much of my behavior, even when I truly thought I was bringing a different person with a new issue to analysis, every time, when we excavated long enough, one way or another they were all Bon Bon.

It was in the garden surrounding Bon Bon's house that I first piddled around in the soil. I had loved watering at my other grandmother's house as a child, but in her effort to avoid the searing Texas summer heat, Grandma always did her actual gardening so early I was never awake for it. I did go out alone, though, and watered her flowers and her trees. She had a rambling wisteria that I adored, and a mimosa with soft, feathery, fragrant blossoms I loved to trace across my face. I have a strong memory of running a stream of cooling water from the hose up and down the bark of the giant pecan tree in her backyard, as high as I could reach with the water, and feeling as if I could sense the soothing effect it was having on the tree. I didn't know how to express it at the time, but I know now the connection was energetic. A perception that I believe comes from something as simple as paying attention. When I paid close attention to the tree, I could feel it.

Bon Bon's garden was different from Grandma's. Bigger to be sure, and not gardened in. No random flowers here and there, no unruly wisteria or shedding mimosas for her. Bon Bon's yard was landscaped. Simple, more elegant. More what the neighbors would expect. Having "made good" in the big city after growing up on a farm in Illinois in the late nineteenth and early twentieth centuries, Bon Bon had no interest whatsoever in engaging in gardening or anything else that resembled farming. Her grounds had the kind of staid, unremarkable feel to them that comes from doing exactly what is required to meet the stature of the house and the prestige of the neighborhood without any personal touch or hint of who might live there. Well taken care of in the way any other check-listed item is dealt with, her garden stood as a monument to meticulously maintained neglect. She had five huge American elm trees on her property, and an enviably lush green lawn, the kind that made you want to run through it barefoot. But acting on one or two such foolhardy impulses revealed a lawn that was booby-trapped with copper sprinkler heads that would rip your feet open, effectively curtailing any further desire to gambol through her green.

Standing in stark contrast to an otherwise completely green landscape, on the far east side of her front flower bed, was a bright blue hydrangea. I can only imagine it was once a potted gift that she had her yardman plant once its blooms faded. Otherwise it made no sense in the landscape. But I loved it. Besides the trees and the lawn, it was the only pretty thing in that yard.

Bon Bon's only child, our father, had died at the age of thirty-two, so when Bon Bon passed away, my sister and I were her only heirs. Her house was a lovely Georgian on an oversized lot in Old Highland Park, a status symbol of which she was very proud. My sister was married and living in California and I had just graduated from college when Bon Bon had a stroke. She died after a brief hospital stay, and I reluctantly moved into her house. Beautiful though the home itself was, moving into the house where I had suffered such terrible treatment was actually quite traumatic, though I didn't fully realize it at the time. I just knew I hated her and hated her house, and it gave me the creeps every time I walked in the door. But it was free, I was young, and I needed a place to live. Plus, she had over half a century of personal belongings that somebody had to deal with, so I moved in.

I lived at Bon Bon's house for over a year, sorting through a lifetime of memories. Hers, mine, and ours. She had always claimed her house was haunted. It certainly was for me. Haunted by every cruel, humiliating, degrading, malevolent thing she ever said to me or put me through. By the time I left, I had made an uneasy peace with the house, if not the woman. When I moved out, I decided to take the blue hydrangea with me. After all, it wasn't the hydrangea's fault it had ended up at Bon Bon's. When I went out to dig it up, and reached into the soil to gather the root ball, I narrowly missed being seriously lacerated by about twenty large, sharp, heavily rusted nails that were buried around it. Booby-trapped again. How typical. I learned later that this was how people turned hydrangeas blue in our local alkaline soil. Back when nails were made of iron, rust from degrading nails acidified the soil, making the natural aluminum more available. But whatever the horticultural reason, what it felt like was one last jab from Bon Bon on my way out. Little did I know the lessons from Bon Bon were only just beginning.

Women Grieve;
Men Replace

About two years into our separation, Daniel invited me to dinner, ostensibly to talk about some financial things, but it turned out the real reason was to tell me about Jane. Daniel and Jane had grown up together. I hear he has a picture of her at his second-grade birthday party. They had reunited at the funeral of an old high school friend, and soon began their affair. Theirs was a long-distance relationship since Jane had moved to the East Coast years before, but she regularly traveled home to Dallas to visit family, and Daniel often had business on the East Coast, so their affair had plenty of time and opportunity to grow. By the time he told me about her, Jane was leaving her husband, moving back to Dallas, and moving in with Daniel. Piecing together small details through the haze of shock over the course of dinner, evidence pointed to the likelihood that Jane had been in the picture since well before Dan and I separated. It was that, not the fact of her, that rocked my world. You see, whenever I told a friend that Daniel had asked me for a divorce, everyone...every single person, either asked if or strongly asserted that he must have someone else. And each and every time, I defended him to the last word, which I always insisted on having.

"No way," I declared definitively. "Daniel has flaws, but he doesn't have that one. He is the most honorable man I have ever known, and he would never, ever do that."

"Men don't leave unless they have someone else," they told me.

"Some men, maybe. But not Daniel." I was absolutely certain of that, and I believed it to my core until the moment he told me I was wrong.

To say this revelation was world shattering sounds like a hyperbolic cliché, but it isn't. It literally splintered and then reshaped my worldview, but not for the obvious reasons. It was a Thursday night, July 3. I remember the date because the next day was the Fourth of July, and the fireworks that exploded over my house felt like cluster bombs. I remember the day because trauma imprints random information that way. I remember that I was poised in the face of this point-blank detonation of my reality. I was proud of myself for that. I was stunned, but I did not react. At least not the way one might expect from such a close-range blast impact.

I asked a few questions.

Was he in love with her? Yes.

Did he plan to marry her? Maybe.

When we left the restaurant, I was quiet as we walked to my car. On reflection, what I experienced as dignified composure on my part was probably just shock. There was more he tried to say, but I stopped him and told him I needed to leave. It was a minuscule gesture of self-care I normally would not have given myself. It felt empowered at the time.

All day the next day, my devastation and panic were rising. Slowly at first, but at an accelerating rate as the hours passed. Difficult though it may be to understand, it had nothing to do with Jane per se. To this day, I have never felt even the tiniest hint of animosity toward her. Indeed, when my thoughts fell in her direction, which didn't happen until much later and then only rarely, I can honestly say the only thing I ever felt for her was gratitude. Both Daniel and I were conflict avoidant and emotionally paralyzed in a feedback loop of inertia. Jane knocked us out of orbit. Had it not been for her, who knows how much longer he and I would have stayed in that miserable marriage. Maybe forever.

But she was irrelevant on this day. From the moment I rose from a sleepless night, my body wailed in existential agony, with deep, sharp pains in places I never even knew existed. I was on the floor of my living room. For hours, my body shook. I was sobbing, convulsing, gasping for air, melting down. I was so overwhelmed with emotion I was at a critical breaking point. I couldn't get away from myself, from my thoughts. I was shorting out emotionally. I had never had an experience like this before, and I couldn't get a handle on anything. Not my feelings, not my thoughts.

The one thing I was sure I knew about Daniel was wrong, and if that was not true, if I didn't even know that one fundamental character trait about the man with whom I had lived for twenty-five years, then what did I know? Who did I know? Anyone? Ever? Who could I trust? Certainly not him. But more importantly, not *me*! Not my own sense of judgment. This reality didn't sink in. It covered me like a plastic body bag cinched tight around my neck. My entire center point of reference about people and the world was ripped out, hanging from me like gutted entrails. I was alone. Floating in an abyss. Everything I thought I knew was wrong, and I was completely, completely lost.

So much of nature happens in soundless slow motion. Lazy-day clichés notwithstanding, one cannot really watch the grass grow or a flower unfurl. But nature's love of contrast also gives us devastating upheaval and destruction on a biblical scale. A year after the catastrophic flash flood of the Blanco River sent a forty-foot-high wall of water crashing through the peaceful country community of Wimberley, Texas, the scars of nature's cataclysmic power still remained, and the air still echoed with loss. Thousands of huge trees, some of them hundreds of years old, were ripped from the ground and shattered like so many brittle twigs. Fresh, tight bark was stripped from the limbless trunks, and massive chunks of concrete and amorphous debris were hurled across the riverbanks, then dropped hundreds of yards away with the dispassion of a petulant child. Homes were ripped from their foundations and thrust into the furious surging river. Innocent lives were lost. The rawness with which nature destroys that which it creates is a lesson we too often forget. The river cared not who or what was in its path. Everything was destroyed. And survivors were not spared; they were just lucky.

The disintegration of my marriage began in quiet slow motion. There were storms, for sure, but on balance, love had seeped away silently, like an unnoticed leak that you realize too late has destroyed the foundation of your home. But this was not that. This was a Category 5 event with a massive storm surge that rose around me faster than I could catch my breath, engulfing my undefended heart. Over the next days and weeks, as I struggled to tread these murky floodwaters of my life, a friend (who graciously did not say, "I told you so") asked me why this news was so devastating. If it wasn't the obvious reason—betrayal, infidelity, and "the other woman"—what was it?

I closed my eyes and let the question pass mind into heart.

Several years prior, a group of friends and I were engaged in a conversation about what was most important to us. Someone turned to me and asked, "What is your most deeply held longing?"

"To be known," I said without hesitation. It wasn't a longing I had thought about much, or ever, to be honest. Not in any real way. But when the words fell from my lips more as reflex than reply, I recognized how true they were. Being known and truly understood was not something I had ever experienced, and it was my deepest longing. All my life I had felt like an outlier. A bit of an alien creature. As I got older and began taking personality tests, I learned that, sure enough, my suspicions proved accurate. In every variation on a testing theme I scored in the category representing the fewest people: Myers-Briggs INFJ; Enneagram Four, and so on.

The first revelation came years ago, when my little garden club had a party that included our husbands. We chose a speaker who was a marriage counselor. She gave us one of these tests as an introduction to her talk. We were all in our late twenties to early thirties, and it was the first personality test I had ever taken. I don't remember which test it was, but I do remember this—both Daniel and I fell into groups that represented only 1 percent of the population, but we were not in the same 1 percent. We thought this was hilarious at the time and started calling ourselves the One Percenters. I realize now we should have paid more attention to this little factoid than we did.

The problem with being a One Percenter is that being known becomes significantly harder since, by definition, 99 percent of the population will not easily get you. Couple that with how my family kept moving around Europe when I was growing up so I never had a chance to form deep, lasting friendships, and the net result was that any sense of aloneness one might naturally feel as an introverted One Percenter was significantly amplified in my life.

With my eyes still closed, I sat in silence. Her question penetrated past tissue, fluid, and bone. Why was this news so devastating? It pierced through thought and passed awareness, landing somewhere in the energetic realm between consciousness and the infinite.

How can we ever really know another person when we do not even truly know ourselves? We think we know ourselves, but that which we are willing to acknowledge is a shiny, polished, idealized version we can accept. A meticulously edited personal narrative that is far from complete and accurate. Any evidence to the contrary, any moments or memories that do not align, are completely denied or dismissed as anomalous and in no way reflective of our true selves.

But the reality is, we are all capable of things both far greater and much more terrible than we will admit. Our Shadows are powerful places of untapped darkness, and untapped light. There are parts of us that are dangerous, even deadly, which we rarely, if ever, express. But when the weight of circumstances grows sufficiently overwhelming, when our life, our reputation, or our wounded inner child is threatened, we all say or do things we cannot believe we have said or done. Things of which we are so ashamed we hide all evidence, or quickly sublimate. We all have secrets and darkness within that we cannot or will not see, leaving enormous gaps in our self-awareness.

If we cannot ever truly know ourselves, then how can we ever truly know anyone else?

And if we can never truly know anyone else, then my deepest, most heartfelt longing—the desire to be known—was impossible. If we are all essentially unknowable, then we are all effectively alone. It was this profound existential truth that tore my soul open to a level of grief I was not sure was survivable. Not only was I alone, but no matter who might come into my life, I would ultimately remain alone.

I had been replaced in Daniel's life, but I felt almost nothing about her.

I was eternally alone, and I felt that in every atom of my being.

Chapter 2

Fallow

I Am Autumn

Fall is breathing its soft, cooling breath into the nights and mornings now, and I can feel myself noticeably relaxing. The relentless heat of Texas summers can be hard for me.

Each morning in the fall, when I open my doors and the cool breeze washes over me, I feel my energy expand. It's a little early in the season yet, but as I take my morning walk through the garden, I have begun to notice tiny hints of fall color peeking around edges of leaves, like anxious actors behind the curtain backstage. I, too, am excited for their time in the limelight. What a glorious treat fall color is. It takes my breath away every year.

And this year, in particular, I welcome the transformation. It has been a year of deep change for me, and it came at a high price—months of personal upheaval, processing, and self-discovery brought on by emotional pain so intense that it felt as if my very life depended on understanding the cause, finding the source, and healing it.

It started in late winter, as the trees were beginning to bud, then intensified through the spring and into the summer as the leaves unfurled and engaged in their annual process of ensuring the survival of their host. We worked in tandem—they nurturing from without, I nurturing from within, scouring the hidden depths of my psyche for understanding. Each of us gathering, storing, distilling, converting, day in and day out through summer's end. And now, as the breakdowns and breakthroughs are coalescing within me, I feel the self that is emerging is more my true self than I have ever been.

In this way, I am Autumn.

The beautiful fresh greens we think of as the natural color of leaves is actually a mask of sorts. It is a sign that the tree is working hard. Green leaves are striving for survival by using the chlorophyll coursing through their veins in the warm spring and summer months. Green leaves are processing and converting sunlight, water, and carbon dioxide into a form that feeds the trees, helps them grow, and can sustain them through the winter. But as the days shorten and sunlight becomes increasingly scarce, nature shifts its focus from gathering and processing food to integrating and storing what has been gathered, transferring it from the leaves to the roots. As this happens, the worker-bee greens drop away and the leaves' true colors begin to emerge. The beautiful, vivid colors of fall are not created; they are revealed.

Most of the time, we are green leaves. We go about our daily routines, striving for survival. We spend our days, and often our nights, coping. Coping with work, with children, with parents, with all the responsibilities that consume our lives, trying to fit in some quality time here and there with our loved ones, and maybe, if we're lucky, with ourselves. We are bright, shiny, busy green leaves, doing what we must to ensure our survival, until one day a crisis hits, and it's impossible to continue with business as usual.

In those moments, we are stripped of our ability to hide behind our busyness and are forced to be fully present with this new reality and find within ourselves the internal fortitude that previously lay dormant. Our lovely green facade disintegrates, and all those pressing goals and demands that have consumed our time and attention day in and day out diminish, and sometimes completely disappear. In moments of personal cataclysm, something wiser, more resilient, more courageous wakes within us, bringing with it the necessary strength to confront our greatest challenges, no matter how harsh. In those moments, we become Autumn. Authentic, unmasked, raw, real, powerful, and beautiful. When crisis strips away our masks and guides us inside to our authentic selves, the beauty it reveals can be staggering. When we are unmasked, we are vibrant; we are radiant. When we are wholly ourselves, it is holy.

Seasons change and so do I, and right now, I am Autumn.

The Itsy Bitsy Spider

It was spring, full on. The flowering quince, the forsythia, and the tulip trees were still in full flourish. Daffodils sprouted under trees in golden swaths. Showers of white spirea cascaded like fairy waterfalls over mossy stone walls and around masses of crystal blue irises so thick and wide and deep it looked as if the sky had decided to lie down and take a rest in my garden.

This colorful morning scene was all the more delightful because a spring storm had blown in overnight, and the temperatures had dipped so much that it was downright chilly, so I decided to build a fire to enjoy with my morning tea. After laying the kindling, I went out to the porch and chose a piñon log, both because they catch more easily and because they smell so lovely when they burn. You can't really smell it in the house that much after the first few minutes, but outside it smells amazing, so I consider it my neighborhood community service.

Just as I was about to toss it into the fire, I noticed a tiny movement along a split ridge in the bark. Looking more closely, I saw a small black spider who had been disturbed when I picked up the log and now seemed to be waiting to see what was going to happen next.

"Well, good morning, little," I said to her as she sat motionless and unsure. "I'm afraid you are going to need to relocate. This property has been condemned."

I took the log outside and tried to shake her off, but she held on tight. I picked up a leaf and shoved her gently, trying to coax her off, but she darted into a crevice. I pounded the end of the log on the porch floor to try to dislodge her, but she was hanging tough. I broke off a small sliver of bark to try to agitate her from her potentially fatal hiding place, but instead of jumping off, she slipped between the bark and the wood where it was very tight and I couldn't reach.

"Oh, you did *not* just do that, did you?! Come out, you little dope! I'm trying to help you," I said out loud.

I decided to put the log down and step away, hoping that when her home stopped moving around, maybe she would emerge on her own to see if the coast was clear. Sure enough, after a few minutes, she took a couple of cautious steps out from the crevice. I stayed still. She moved a few more tentative steps out, all the way into the open, and I quickly brushed her off the log and onto the porch floor with a long iris leaf. She circled several times, apparently disoriented.

"I'm sorry, honey," I said. "You're going to have to find another home, but you have no idea how much worse it almost was for you."

I walked inside and plopped the log onto the fire, and as I did, I started thinking about all the times in my life when I had clung to something or someone as if my life depended on it, not realizing until much later that what my life really depended on was letting go. I thought about how many times the big scary power that appeared to be pushing me mercilessly out of my comfort zone was really the hand of God guiding me to safety, right before my old life was about to burst into flames. I thought about how that spider would never understand that I was saving her life, but that she, in her little metaphorical spidery way, had helped to remind me to trust in the process, to release my grip, and to always watch for each and every tiny affirmation that, even in the midst of upheaval, all is well. All is well.

First Touch

Glenn and I had been friends online for a few years when he first told me he was in love with me. I was charmed and flattered, but since he was significantly younger than I, I had initially dismissed his ardor as nothing more than a crush of youth. We had met on a website where we were both community forum moderators. He was extremely kind and supportive of me when I would confide insecurities about myself and my future, and his attention and interest in my life felt warm and comforting in unfamiliar ways after years of rejection in an unhappy marriage. Still uncomfortable with the semiavailable status of separation, I was resistant when he shared his feelings, yet I couldn't help but realize how much I needed to hear those words from someone. After years of enduring my husband's resentments blowing out sideways in the form of constant criticism about everything from my weight, to my clothes, to my weight, to my personal habits, to my weight, to my housekeeping, to my weight, to how I spent money, to my weight, I had long ago forgotten what it felt like to be admired. But the memory of this distant sensation was stirred by Glenn's kindness, and I found my heart becoming increasingly fertile ground for someone who saw more in me than just my weight, my seemingly infinite flaws, and my myriad perceived failings.

If, as the early twentieth-century English journalist Cyril Connolly once wrote, "the true index of a man's character is the health of his wife," then Dan had a lot to learn. In the years leading up to our separation, I had devolved into an emotional wreck, the evidence of which was showing up in my body in numerous ways with multiple random symptoms both common and obscure, including but not limited to protective weight gain, sexual issues, recurring depression, and medical oddities like spontaneous purple hickey-like bruising on my extremities, and irregular tonsil regrowth that quickly became so severe it had blocked two-thirds of my throat and required surgery. Mind-body connection advocates would say those last two in particular were no coincidence for someone enduring constant verbal denigration and who was so disempowered she had completely lost her voice in her primary relationship.

Some years before, on a trip to Sedona, Arizona, as I stood at the base of a massive red rock formation, surrounded by gigantic boulders the size of small houses which had once been hundreds of feet above, I remember thinking,

"In the face of constant erosion, and with insufficient support, even mountains eventually crumble." As did I.

For at least a couple of years before he moved out, Daniel had been spending as much time as possible away from home, and had long since ceased to say goodbye when he left. I would look up and he would be gone with no word of where he was going or when he might return, leaving me feeling increasingly invisible and micro-abandoned on a daily basis. I finally stopped asking where he had been for the past many hours, after the thousandth time he said, "I was just driving around." For more years than I care to remember, my husband had looked at me alternately with frustration, indifference, and contempt.

Glenn, on the other hand, saw more beauty, wisdom, and lovability in me than I had ever seen in myself. Glenn messaged me first thing every morning and rushed home every day to talk to me. He spent hours with me online and on the phone. Glenn thought I was lovely and witty and wonderful in every way possible, and the more I opened myself to him, the deeper and more effusive his love and admiration grew. My many foibles, which Daniel saw as fundamental failures of character and effort, Glenn saw as tender vulnerabilities to be cared for, nurtured, and protected. What Daniel saw as weakness, Glenn saw as delicate and poetic. My fragilities balanced my strengths in his eyes. He saw both. He treasured both. Because of this, in time, I grew to feel safer with him than I had ever felt with anyone.

There was an added layer of complexity (or was it simplicity?) to the refuge Glenn was creating in my life. He

63

lived in Toronto. I was in Dallas. We had never met in person. As odd and out of the parameters of my experience as this was, I believe his lack of proximity was an integral part of why we worked so well at first. It was easy for me to compartmentalize our friendship and hold it solely as such, without the pressure and confusion a budding relationship could cause had it been local, potentially creating more problems than it solved.

It would be three more years until we met in person, but in ways I could never have predicted, this lack of proximity was an invisible safety net for me. I was able to "practice" and relearn what it meant to share loving energy and kindness with a member of the opposite sex, without the perils of actually having to act on it. This virtual relationship gave me a sense of being valued while simultaneously protecting me from the triggers of my deeply wounded distrust of the masculine. My life experience and wisdom had value for Glenn, while his youth and sweet guilelessness were nonthreatening and healing to me. It was a hybridized relationship, like a rose bred for form but not fragrance. It was beautiful, but incomplete. Yet it was safe, which at the time was what mattered most to me.

Bright White
Nights

Late in the evenings, just before midnight, I can usually be found venturing out to my garden and into the steaming spa waters at the end of my pool. I have probably been in my spa 75 to 80 percent of the nights since I bought this house. Whether the weather is mild in the spring, hot in the summer, freezing in the winter, or bringing a chill in the fall, I love to go out into the quiet night and let my cares be washed away by the gently churning water and the sparkling night sky. I am so comfortable with nighttime's indigo veil over my garden, it is as familiar to me as any other part of my home. But every once in a while, when I go out for my midnight swim, I feel as if I have entered a different painting.

On the rather rare occasions when there are rain clouds

high but not too dense between me and a full or nearly full moon, instead of a dark night, there is a white one. Lit from behind like a fashion photographer's light box, the whole sky becomes a white scrim illuminating the garden with a diffuse glow bright enough to see all the way to the property's edge. Bare trees become black skeletons against the white night sky, and the whole garden transforms into line and form on canvas.

White nights remind me of the perpetual twilight of summer eves during my childhood years in Scotland, and the nights Dan and I spent on a rather adventurous trip we took to the USSR in the midst of the Cold War. Those summer nights in Leningrad, we joined locals walking the city until three, four, or five in the morning without the need of streetlights or the Pavlovian weariness that comes with awareness that the sun has set hours before. Time is elastic when it's not defined by light. There was only the endless, eerie umbrella of pink, a sunset that refused to let go and sleep, conjoined as it was with the sunrise.

Seeing my garden colorless, as only form and texture, I notice things normally unseen. Intricacies of structure, undulations of conformity interrupted by moments of independence, patterns of light in negative space that become focal in the bright white night. It reminds me of a Mondrian retrospective I once saw at the Guggenheim Museum in New York City. Early in his career as an artist, Mondrian painted from nature, particularly trees. Over time, his trees became more and more stylized as he searched for the purest form of abstraction in his art, eventually reducing his subjects down to their most essential elements of line and its corresponding negative space.

This stripped-down perspective is a doorway to deeper understanding and appreciation of ourselves. The lines are our thoughts and beliefs, our conscious minds. Everything else, our unconscious and subconscious, is the negative space. And it is vast. Looking again to Mondrian, it is in the spaces between the structure, the lines, where we find color. Bold, clear, primary, emphatic color. Similarly, our creativity, our inspiration, our brilliance, everything that makes us bright and unique, all of our potential is found in the spaces outside of and around the constraints of our conditioning and our training; the grid of our thoughts, our assumptions, our beliefs. Our greatest potential and every new, innovative idea we will ever have lies beyond existing rules of what we've been taught, who we think we are, and what we think we know.

Looking at the garden in daylight, our eye is drawn to the colors, shadings, and movements of each plant, flower, tree, and inhabitant. The birds, the lizards, the insects, each petal, leaf, and twig—how we see all these things is affected by the quality, intensity, and direction of the light. But in its absence, we are invited to notice line, form, and the void. I am drawn to the void. I want to see what's beyond my parameters. I want to know what wisdom is to be found in the empty space into which I feel called to grow. I want to meet my Shadow and learn from it. I want to unbury and acknowledge the parts of me that are dark, and liberate the parts of me that are so powerfully light they frighten me.

I have been erased and redrawn, again and again, by the hand of life. Like an imperfect Galatea, each time I reemerge, still misshapen from sadness, disproportioned by wounds, fragile from abandonment and betrayal. But this time I intend to take the pencil into my own hand. Carl Jung wrote, "Until you make the unconscious conscious, it will direct your life and you will call it fate." I am finished with that feckless cop-out. I want to understand.

Each time I go outside to find a rare white night, I think of the line "The sky sure is white" from that depressing little Tennessee Williams one-act play *This Property Is Condemned*. But unlike Alva, whose fanciful delusions dissociated her from her brief, tragic life and infected her little sister's worldview, I choose to acknowledge the events that have shaped me. I intend to transcend my wounding. I will make my unconscious conscious. I will call fate by my name.

Opposites Attract

The high desert around Santa Fe and Taos, New Mexico, is a study in contrasts. It gets scorching hot and bitter cold. It is mostly dry, but it also snows, and when it rains, the monsoons send torrents of water hard and fast that come suddenly and end just as abruptly. The land can be so expansive and flat in one direction you can see all the way to the earth's horizon. In another direction, it might be broken by mesas and mountains rugged, bare, and foreboding. And around the next corner, mountains rise and fall with deep, gentle, fluid ripples as warm and wise as the faces of its elderly native inhabitants. Even the words *high desert* themselves seem a contradiction in terms.

High desert conditions are harsh, but the colors are soft. Whisper-pale terracotta and blush-colored earth is interrupted only sporadically by the silver blues of scrubby wild sage and chamisa. Dead and dying shrubs, trees, and grasses, bleached by the sun and drained of life-giving nutrients, are ghostly gray, yet blend so seamlessly they are often indistinguishable from their living counterparts. The muted shades of yucca, agave, cactus, and cholla, more celadon than true green, are further softened by spines, hairs, and fuzzy or waxy coatings that protect them from dramatically changing weather as well as munching invaders. Indeed, few plants are truly green in these deserts, and the cool shades of aqua, blue, silver, gray, and white that predominate the plant palette are as iconic as the undulating warm adobe structures they surround.

This quiet, muted earthen canvas provides the foundation for some pretty raucous color events as the days begin and end. Without a natural dominance of texture or color, the mountains and plains here reflect the changing colors of the sky with great enthusiasm. Whereas heavily green, forested landscapes absorb much of the color of the emerging or waning day, the southwestern desert amplifies and enhances it. Mountains have luminous golden peaks that morph into vivid shades of rose, orange, and red. The Sangre de Cristo range is named the Blood of Christ for this very phenomenon, as the mountains briefly transform into monuments of deep crimson at the beginning and end of each day. This earth, shell pink and unobtrusive by day, ignites into a fluorescent concert of color as the sun sinks in the west. Light does not easily give way to darkness here. It seizes the senses one last time with a flood of amber incandescence that races across the land. In its wake, each spiny, bristly, aggressively defended plant is momentarily transformed. In these brief moments of diagonal light, each rugged plant ceases to be armored. Instead, in a twice-daily celestial anointing, the spines along every line, curve, and contour of the chollas, cactuses, and grasses catch the light and transmute into glowing, luminous, bright white halos. It is so strange how this barren, seemingly hostile land softens in the angled light of dusk and dawn. It begs recognition. To be seen in a different light. It is beautiful, and it wants you to know that its defenses do not define it.

My defenses do not define me, either, though I know that's not always apparent. My wounded thorns and spines are invisible. I was never beaten. Nothing shows. But great suffering unseen is still great suffering. And in the same way that an animal who has been abused reflexively recoils even from a hand raised without threat, my throat clamps shut when I feel harshly or unfairly criticized, and I eat reflexively when I'm afraid.

Glenn always saw me in that different light. A light far kinder than I was used to being seen in, especially for the last eight or ten years of my marriage. Glenn never saw the thorns or spines surrounding me as aggressive. Like the radiant cholla at sunset in Joshua Tree, he only ever saw them as a halo. Starved for unconditional affection and validation, when Glenn showered me with adoration and effusive words of love, I wanted to believe him and receive every expression of his passion, but instead I was more like the drought-hardened clay soils of north Texas than the receptive arms of love. After baking in the sun and scorching heat of summer with little or no relief from rain, the clay soil in Texas solidifies. Sometimes, it hardens so much that when rain finally does fall, the soil repels the very water it so desperately needs rather than absorbing it. I know I did the same thing with Glenn. His love was more than I could absorb for a long time. But he never took it personally nor held that against me. He just loved me no matter what. I had a lot to recover from after my marriage, and it was his absolute pleasure to steady me on that road.

One night, on the phone, I was spinning out about something that had nothing to do with him. Angry and venting, I was looking for a target. He was fairly quiet on the other end of the line, so I turned my sights on him.

"What's the matter? Why aren't you saying anything?" I snapped.

"I'm sorry," he said, unruffled by my tone. "I wasn't talking because I was focusing my energy on you, trying to help ground you."

In that moment, every drop of anger I felt evaporated. Even though he was fifteen hundred miles away, I had never felt so lovingly held.

Glenn's voice was the most effective antianxiety treatment on earth for me. There was a tone of voice I knew he only used with me. A voice that resonated with love and understanding like a soft chorus under every word. Sometimes I would call him and ask him to talk to me. It didn't matter what he said. I just needed to hear the deep, resonant, soothing wave of sounds only he could make.

Reflecting on my internal resistance to this beautiful

young man, I now know that his age, which I always used as a reason not to commit, was also the very reason to commit. Deeply disempowered with the masculine my whole life, with Glenn, I had de facto power, simply by virtue of our age difference. I didn't realize it for most of our time together, but the early stages of my healing around the masculine at large was due in great part to the ease with which I could assert myself with Glenn. An ease borne from a combination of his completely unrestrained, nonjudgmental love, his youth, and his utter lack of attachment to holding all the power. He had no problem with my having power, which was a whole new experience in my life. But even as I tried to restrict his access to my heart, his gentle patience and persistence was like a stream creating a canyon, with an unwavering insistence that we were one—soul mates—and always had been. One night in yet another vain attempt to explain to him the Problem with Us, I said, "You know, in twenty years, you are going to be in the prime of your life, and I am going to be *really* old." To which he replied, "I can think of no greater honor than to be by your side until the moment you transition this earth."

This was not the soul of youth. Glenn was only young chronologically.

The foliage on high desert plants is typically small, thin, and rugged. This is what happens over time when conditions are relentlessly harsh. For desert plants, this prevents excessive moisture loss and damage from sun scorch, ripping wind, and the weight of ice and snow. But this lack of surface area also restricts what plants can receive, and so it was for me. All my love and acceptance receptors had been reduced to bare survival proportions, and Glenn was a monsoon of love. I was damaged, but at some level, I was willing—no, desperate—to be so adored. I struggled with his devotion in ways he never knew and could likely never understand. How could he? His love was so deep, so absolute, it would have been inconceivable for him to imagine a world in which we were not together, happily ever after. A shameless romantic, he recorded himself reading love poems to me and sent me the lyrics to love songs. He loved to adorn me with beautiful hair accessories and jewelry. He sent flowers—so many flowers. We had *songs*. I had never been with anyone romantic enough to admit we had songs. I had had songs in other relationships, but *we* never did. But Glenn wanted the fairy tale. The fairy tale I had long since given up on. So when he came into my life, my task was to learn how to accept the kind of romantic love I had always wanted, and he had to give.

The wounded skeptic in me didn't even believe in this kind of infatuation infused love, but I wanted to believe that true, lasting love could grow from the seeds of such romance. And I wanted—deeply wanted—to try to let the kind of love Glenn offered take root and blossom, despite all my efforts to stunt it.

I'm complicated, but at least I know it.

In many ways, Glenn and I were opposites, but in other ways we were so similar. More than similar, really. In many ways we were the same. Tender, sensitive, wounded, heart-centered, demonstrative souls who had been misunderstood and mistreated. Against geography, chronology, societal norms, and all odds or logic, we found each other in a corner of the world so obscure, it could only be described as destiny.

The Lifeline

Each year in the spring there is a period of a few weeks when the wolf spiders in my garden decide to go for a swim. Nearly every morning I can find at least one spider in my pool—sometimes floating, sometimes completely submerged on the walls of the pool or on a step, and each time, I quickly find a leaf or a branch and rush to reach a lifeline to the poor things, fishing them out and returning them to the safety of dry land.

Now, mind you, I've never seen one of them struggling or looking distressed in any way. I do occasionally find some that are dead, but those are a tiny percentage compared to how many I find alive and well, even though some have been underwater for goodness knows how long.

Recently, now that spider saving season is here again,

I've been thinking about this annual ritual. Why do these spiders go into the pool every year? Why only during this one time of year? How do some of them appear to be able to breathe underwater or at least hold their breath for very extended periods of time? And if they can hold their breath for long periods, why do some of them die?

These questions all came from the naturalist in me. The endless, insatiable desire to understand the natural world around me. The animated curiosity I always feel when a question occurs to me about how and why nature works the way it does.

But then a different set of questions began to seep into my consciousness. Why do I assume these spiders are in danger? Why do I feel the need to save them? Do they really need to be saved? Am I even helping?

These questions came from a different place inside me. A deeper place. The place that longs to understand what makes *me* work the way I do. When I stretch a lifeline out to these spiders, they each grab it in what I interpret as relief, but am I just projecting? Is it instinct rather than emotion that grabs the leaf? Who really needs to be saved? Who feels adrift? Who has been holding their breath for goodness knows how long? Who feels submerged, underwater, overwhelmed? Who is really crying out for a lifeline?

Humans have developed a habit of thinking they know more than nature, and we've done a lot of damage because of that hubris. A case in point being how we used to handle forest fires.

The common wisdom was to prevent all forest fires at

all costs. Period. We decided forest fires were bad, so the logic was to stop them all. Until one day someone figured out that forest fires were simply not completely preventable. Whether it be from campfires accidentally getting out of control, from lightning strikes, or from arson, forest fires are going to happen, but if they have been efficiently prevented from occurring naturally for years or even decades, a terrible thing follows. When the inevitable forest fire finally breaks out, there is significantly more accumulated debris and ignitable material on the forest floor. This provides an unnatural amount of fuel for the fire, causing it to burn hotter and longer, spread faster, and become more dangerous than nature would have allowed had she not been interfered with in the first place. We have seen this heartbreaking reality in California and other places in the west, south, and southwest. The truth is, forest fires are a part of nature's design. They are not all bad. They are a powerful and important part of earth's natural cycles. What makes them so dangerous now is our encroachment into the forest, causing fires to be a threat to human lives. This is the conundrum we continue to create as we overtake more and more wild land.

Along the same lines, but from the opposite end of the spectrum, focused efforts to eliminate rattlesnakes or other predators have resulted in some areas being overrun by rodents that would have been naturally controlled by these "dangerous" predators. The same is true of the deer population. Had we not decimated their natural predators such as cougars, bobcats, wolves, and coyotes, the deer population would never get out of control.

Of course, my little spider saving ritual does not interfere with nature on the scale of forest fires or mass snake killings, but it is similar in that it comes from an essential belief that interfering with the natural order and cycle of life is something I am qualified to do. And it is something I believe I am qualified to do because I am making assumptions about the situation that may or may not be accurate. What if this foray into a body of water is a necessary part of their mating habits? Or what if these are mother spiders drawing up water for their eggs? I looked in the pool and saw spiders in the water as spiders in danger. Spiders who needed to be saved. Kind of like those people whose own lives are in a shambles but who are so quick to offer advice to others rather than really looking at their own stuff. Annoying, right? I didn't understand why those spiders were in the water and I was not comfortable with it, so I overlaid my own fears onto them and declared them spiders in danger who needed my help. I endowed them with my sense of peril because my survival feels threatened, and if I'm honest, deep down I desperately want to be saved.

When my husband told me he wanted to divorce, he said he would take care of me for as long as I needed until I could get on my feet financially. This gesture was partially because he is fundamentally a genuinely good guy. I'm also fairly certain it was also partially because he felt guilty. Of course, I appreciated it because he certainly didn't have to do that, and since I was paralyzed with fear and self-doubt, with no idea how I would take care of myself, I don't know what I would have done if he had launched straight into divorce proceedings. That being said, after over a decade of anger and resentment building inside me because of how he blamed me for everything short of the national debt, another part of me thought, "You're damn right you will. It's the least you can do." I was neck-deep in fear and knee-deep in blame, so I crossed my arms and held my breath, planted my heels in the ground, and flatly refused to move forward with my life. That'll show him.

At some level, every time I saved a spider, a tiny block in the foundation of my belief in a safe world was placed. But it didn't really make my world any safer. I could trust my ability to save these tiny creatures, but I had no confidence in my ability to save myself. So I saved what I could and suppressed my real fears about my own survival.

But what if I could take that fear and turn it around? What if I could acknowledge my worry and fear about my ability to take care of myself, fashion it into my own lifeline, lash it around my waist, and haul myself into the only true safe harbor, which is a courageous, daring belief in myself? The last time I reached in to save a spider, a thought occurred to me: "Just because I am floating does not mean I am adrift." Now there's a pearl of truth.

I expect I shall continue to "save" the spiders I find in my pool, but from now on, I'm going to try to remind myself each time I do that all who wander are not lost, all who float are not adrift, and I can take care of myself.

I hope.

Moments of Joy

The oppressive heat of summer has finally broken, and I am able to resume one of my favorite morning rituals: opening the glass double doors in my living room to the garden. This morning, however, was different. This morning, as the doors swung open, the sweep of air they caused was heavy with fragrance. As the relentless, punishing heat of summer had given way to fall, the roses in my garden flushed out. I could see this every time I looked outside. What had changed was that at some point, quietly over time, the roses had reached a critical mass and held enough blooms that the fragrance now reached all the way to my house. It was so unexpected I caught my breath and exclaimed aloud, "Oh my gosh, what *is* that?!" But then, of course, I instantly knew. Nothing smells quite like roses.

I took my tea into the garden and let the fragrance surround me, carried on the soft morning breeze. I was deeply moved by this moment of beauty, and as I sat very still and allowed myself the sensual pleasure that was being carried on each breath of air, I realized something. Moments of joy surround us. This endless striving in the pursuit of joy deprives us of exactly that which we seek. It is the ability and willingness to find moments of joy in what is right before us that ensures we will find it. Believing joy is somewhere "out there" and focusing our effort and attention on trying to find it closes off joy rather than revealing it and is the path to frustration and disappointment. Our attachment to what we think we need to make us happy puts a veil over our ability to see the beauty of what is actually present. I knew I had dozens of rosebushes in my garden that bore thousands if not tens of thousands of blooms, but I thought I knew this particular variety of roses was only faintly fragrant. Not nearly fragrant enough to be enjoyed all the way up to my house. I thought I knew the capacity of these roses, but I was wrong. Nature has no knowledge of our sense of limitation and therefore goes about her business of full expression without our help or hindrance, blithely oblivious to our expectations, or lack thereof.

Thank goodness nature doesn't look to us to fulfill its potential. Think how much smaller it would be. Would we ever imagine the majesty of Niagara Falls, the masses of glorious electric purple blooms on a jacaranda tree, or the exquisite minuscule grass flowers that cover the meadows? Could we have ever dreamed that heat, pressure, and time could transform simple rocks into sparkling gemstones? Looking at our own lives, can we see the seeds of magnificence? Or do our eyes only see that potential to exist in the lives of others? We are all expressions of the same creation. We all possess the ability to achieve greatness. We are all full of potential that perhaps no one else sees, but that exists within us nonetheless. It doesn't matter what others think we can or cannot do. It is our job to bring forth our greatest expression. Our job to see ourselves as more magnificent than others see us. Our job to take their breath away with the wondrous lives we create for ourselves.

Yes, it's a good thing my roses weren't constrained by trying to live up to my paltry expectations. If they had been, I would have completely missed this moment of joy and inspiration.

Letting Go

I have trouble letting go. Letting go of people, property, memories, hurts. I hold on to lots of things I don't need—things that perhaps I have never needed but I keep because someone gave them to me, or I bought them and then realized I didn't need them but was somehow embarrassed to return them. Or far too frequently, because I inherited them. One way or another, they landed in my possession, so I held on to them. I especially hold on to people. I hold on to people long past the time when they were enriching to my life, long past the time when they have an even vaguely positive influence in my life, even past when they have become cruel and destructive. I hold on because, well...I have trouble letting go.

Based on my history, it's not really surprising that I

would have trouble letting go. Having lost some of the most important people in my life through sudden tragedy, it's understandable that I might cling unduly to things I value, especially to living things and most especially to people. But it's not healthy. To be honest, I often feel burdened by the things I have that I don't really want or use, even though they are beautiful and some of them are quite valuable. And I very often wish I could more easily release the relationships that no longer feel supportive. But of all the things I want to let go of, the one I want to let go of the most is this resistance to letting go. I really, really want that. So guess what? I keep getting presented with opportunities to learn to let go, because my soul longs to be free, and this holding on is holding me down.

One of those opportunities presented itself last summer as I was walking through my garden. It came in the form of an unusual cluster of leaves and blooms on one of my rosebushes. I had never seen anything resembling it before. It was about the size of a basketball, with masses of buds and blooms, and reddish leaves that looked like new growth. I thought it was pretty. It was like a complete bridal bouquet thrust out of an otherwise normal rosebush. I noticed it, admired it, then didn't think too much more about it as I went on with my day.

Over the next few months, I noticed more of the rose clusters, and it passed through my mind that they were a little strange, but everything about my roses seemed healthy and beautiful, so once again, I didn't think too much about it. Until one day, I had an arborist out to take care of my trees and he said, "Oh, I see you've got that rose disease. Too bad..."

"What rose disease?" I asked.

"You know—that one that kills the roses."

"I don't know! What one that kills the roses?!"

"Rose rosette," he said.

Rose rosette. I had never heard of it. As soon as he left, I ran inside and searched the internet for rose rosette disease. The news couldn't have been worse. It is a virus carried by minuscule, wingless mites that move from plant to plant on the wind. When a mite carrying the virus infects a rose, the disease becomes systemic, then travels through the plant's vascular system into its roots. From there it can also transfer infection through root contact. It is highly contagious and untreatable. There are no preventative measures, and it kills the rose within approximately two years.

I stared at the computer screen, stunned. The very foundation of my little half-acre garden was roses. I had banks of them. Most were six to eight feet high and just as wide. They were the hallmark of my garden. They defined it. And suddenly, they were all doomed. The whole landscape of my garden as I knew it would soon be unrecognizable. I was devastated. I couldn't believe it. I searched and searched online for some hope of a cure or prevention I could use to save at least some of the rest of my roses, but no, there was not a single word of hope to be found. Nothing. I began to sob, and over the course of the next few days and weeks, I went through all the Kübler-Ross stages of grief: denial, anger, bargaining, depression, and only now, months later, I am finally touching on acceptance.

Buddhism teaches that all suffering comes from attachment. Attachment to people, to places, to things, to relationships, to status, to assumptions, to expectations, to the way we think things ought to be and the way we think people ought to act. Being something of an expert on attachment, I will affirm this to be true for myself. It is definitely my inability to unhook from the people, houses, events, and icons of my past and present that causes me the most ongoing pain. And for what? Nothing has meaning except that which we give to it. But humans are meaning-seeking, meaning-making creatures. I am absolutely inundated with meaningful stuff, and if it has meaning, by golly, I feel compelled to keep it. Even if it doesn't really have meaning for me personally, if it had meaning to someone I loved, then by extension that makes it meaningful to me. But what does all this meaning mean? Does any of it really mean anything?

In the case of the impending loss of my roses, the thread was this: I was looking at the possibility of having to give up my home whenever Daniel and I got around to divorcing. A large part of my attachment to my house, most of it in fact, was my garden. It's easy enough to make a house my own, but it takes years for a garden to grow in, and over the years I had lived there, my garden had reached stunning maturity and had become a sanctuary of spiritual and emotional refuge. With time and care the rose plantings around and throughout my garden had grown into half a dozen private nooks and garden "rooms," each one secluded from the others, quietly waiting to be discovered around the corners of rose walls, through arbors draped with wisteria, and under the outrageous, massive, arched trumpet vine tunnel. Small, fragrant hideaways offering solitude and a place to retreat from the stresses and burdens of my life. Perfect little cloisters of floriferous seclusion with no intrusions save for birds, butterflies, and the occasional bunny. I had fought the prospect of losing my house, because I didn't want to lose my garden, even though some financial advisers had presented the idea that perhaps keeping the house was not the best thing for me to do for reasons less emotional than the thought of losing my garden. But I dismissed their suggestions and professional expertise. They didn't understand about my garden.

But now I was going to lose the showiest, most beautiful part of the garden anyway. So I thought about that. I thought about what it meant to even consider this garden as mine. I thought about how I often say that gardening is a constant lesson in letting go, and a continual reminder that we are not in control. (I would like to take a moment to say how much I hate it when my own words come back to haunt me.) I thought about what different perspectives might now exist and what options they could offer me. What if I didn't think of it as a loss at all? Where was the opportunity? If the bad news was that I was losing my garden, what was the good news? I thought about all this between the tears and the futile attempts to amputate what I once thought were beautiful rose clusters that were now hideous reminders of the imminent death of my roses.

Sometimes it's harder than others to find the gifts in heartbreak. This was one of those times for me. But here's what I came up with: I had never fully designed my own garden. Indeed, for years I'd called it the test garden, because I always bought random plants that were fun, pretty, new, or unusual just to try them out. With very little thought and no plan at all, I would stick them somewhere vaguely appropriate in the garden. In contrast to all those beautiful, award-winning gardens I had designed for other people, mine was, well...a bit of a hodgepodge. A beautiful hodgepodge and one that I loved, but a hodgepodge nonetheless. So what if I got a new blank slate and could design my own garden? How fun would that be?

Less optimistic, but just as real: If I ultimately had to give up my house in the divorce, it would be easier if I weren't also leaving my beloved garden. With the roses gone, I could redo the garden before I put the house on the market, but it would sell long before the new garden had time to grow in enough for me to really fall in love with it.

So, with these two fresh perspectives in mind—one where I got to keep the house and create perhaps an even more lovable garden, and one where the loss of the garden facilitated a more peaceful transition to releasing the house—I took a deep breath and said goodbye to the garden of my inspiration for the last six years. The garden where I drank my tea every morning. The garden where I sought refuge and answers as I healed my shattered spirit and my broken heart. The garden that was featured by HGTV. The garden where I first began to notice parallels between moments in nature and issues in my life, and to write about them.

My heart is willing to let this go if I must. This and all the meaning I have attached to it. When the time comes and a decision has to be made, I am willing to release this house if necessary, and if it is for the best, I am willing to release this garden. And I trust the best is yet to be.

Total Annihilation

Gardening is hard in Texas. The soil is poor and the weather is harsh. It gets really, really hot and it can get really cold, too. Summers can have as many as fifty to sixty days over 100 degrees here, and I can remember days when 105 felt measurably cooler after a few days of over 110. The deep cold doesn't happen that often, and it never lasts more than a few days at a time, but temperatures in the twenties, teens, and even single digits do happen a few times each winter. The problem, however, is not really that it gets so hot here, and it's not that it gets so cold. The problem is that it can do both of those things in the same day. Many is the time I have been alerted on a 75–80 degree day of an impending Blue Norther (which they now more menacingly call a polar vortex). The arctic blast will be heading our way with predicted temperatures plummeting into the teens by nighttime. This kind of drop of forty, fifty, even sixty degrees in a matter of a couple of hours is brutal on plants. Without a chance to harden off or prepare in any way, many otherwise healthy, happy, well-adapted plants will perish in such sudden extremes.

Marriage is hard, too. And not just in Texas. What we want and what we thought we were getting often turn out to be so dramatically different from what we end up with that it can be like living in Bizarro World. Perhaps it was not the man, not the choice, not the circumstances, not the marriage that failed, but the fallacy of the original expectation. Just like the *Camellia japonicas* that nurseries bring in from Monrovia every year. Even though 99.999 percent of them do not survive more than a few seasons here, the lure of the luscious *C. japonica* covered in buds with a few teaser blooms full of promise, its dark, dense, waxy foliage, and its obvious thriving health is irresistible. Likewise, everything about the person we marry appears to be perfect, healthy, and ripe with the assurance of a happily ever after. I don't know about you, but I thought I was marrying the perfect guy. In fact, I called him the Perfect Person for years. My mother, who was not one to give unsolicited advice, once broke her restraint and said, "Darling, you know, that's an awfully high pedestal you've got him up on. It's a long way to fall."

"Well, that would only be a problem if he were going to fall, now, wouldn't it?" I replied glibly.

The more fool I, as Mama would say.

When I'm designing gardens for people, they will often

ask me about camellias, especially if they themselves are transplants from the Deep South. When they do, they are always talking about those gorgeous southern glory shrubs that grow to be twelve to fifteen feet tall and are covered with huge, very double, surreally perfect blooms that graced corsages of old. The japonicas.

"Yes," I will tell them, "you will see those here in nurseries, and every once in a while, you might see one that has found its happy place in a garden, but for the most part, they don't grow well here."

The camellia lover will push. "But I see them in nurseries all the time."

"Yes," I tell them, "but those just arrived from Monrovia. That's in California, where everything grows. Give them a season or two here, and chances are they will be dead."

"Are you sure? They look so pretty at the nursery..."

"Yes," I say, "I am sure."

I confess, I myself have succumbed many times to the allure of a blooming *C. japonica* at a nursery. "Perhaps," I convince myself, "they have developed a variety that will survive here. I'll get this gorgeous thing and give it a go, just one more time." I know better than to do this. I have known better for twenty-five years, and yet I have done this recently. Indeed, I have one dying in my garden at this very moment, even as I write this.

Do as I say, not as I do.

Here's what happens with *Camellia japonicas* in Dallas: They establish slowly and reluctantly in our heavy, alkaline, clay soil. I understand that. It's not their preferred environment. But, they establish slowly and reluctantly, even if you completely excavate the native soil and replace it with beautiful acidic garden soil rich in organic matter. That one, I cannot explain. Should they miraculously survive long enough, they will set their buds in our nice mild winters. Then, if the plant is sufficiently content, and you are incredibly lucky, right around mid-January, it might have a few buds. If you have won the *C. japonica* lottery, it might even be covered with buds, and those buds will begin to grow fat. Really fat. Fatter than seems proportionate to the shrub. And succulent. Oh my goodness, these are the fattest, juiciest, most succulent buds imaginable. They are the double-rich cheesecake of the botanical world. The triple creme brie buds. The death-by-chocolate flourless torte buds. When these ridiculously sumptuous buds get to be about the size of a duck egg, they will begin to push out a little color at the tip. By now the buds are so big and delicious, they scintillate. They titillate. The anticipation of what this plant will be when it is covered in blossoms is intoxicating. Soon, my hapless camellia lover, you are all in. You will go out to the garden multiple times a day, watching for the magnificence that is about to happen. You will plan a garden party around the anticipated bloom time of the camellias. January in Dallas seduces both garden and gardener with warm days, sometimes reaching into the seventies. The buds swell to grander, riper proportions each day. This is it! In a few days those buds are going to open up, and the wonder that is a camellia in full flourish will be yours!

And then, out of nowhere, a Blue Norther blows in and freezes those beautiful buds into crispy little critters. Freezes 'em right through your Plankets. All those fat, glorious, just-about-to-bloom buds will turn brown and mushy, and within a day or two they will all drop off. And you, dear camellia lover, will have to go to bed for a week just to recover from the horticultural heartbreak.

As I percolate in this extended separation from my marriage, I have been thinking a lot about where it derailed. Of course, there are many places, but I truly believe my mother saw it coming before Dan and I ever married. What she saw was my reliance on him to make me happy. She saw me idolize him in a way that was not healthy. She saw me projecting my own light onto him. The light within me that I was afraid of and kept unacknowledged and safely hidden in my Shadow—I had endowed Dan with all of it. She saw me burdening him with the responsibility of my salvation. She saw me, in effect, completely abdicating responsibility for my own happiness and handing it squarely over to him, tenuously held in my projection of his perfection, and all the expectations that came with that. My expectations of perfect love, perfect home, perfect income, perfect life, perfect affection, perfect communication, perfect sex, perfect everything. This was what I expected, not only from the man, but also from the marriage. I was sure that when we were married, everything would fall into place and our perfect love and perfect life would manifest perfectly.

Instead, what I got was a rude awakening of the most

painful kind. Guess what? He wasn't perfect. And our marriage did not bloom as if it had just gotten off the truck from Monrovia for long before the reality of our individual flaws and our mutually flawed expectations took hold.

Where did we derail? From day one. We never really had a shot because our whole relationship was built on a false premise. We each thought the other could make us happy. We each thought the other *did* make us happy. But that was never true. That *is* never true. No other person ever makes us happy. Not really. Not in a healthy, sustainable way. And when unrealistic expectations inevitably meet reality, the result is usually disappointment at a minimum, and often worse: anger, blame, and a sense of betrayal and victimhood.

As my realizations around my fundamental contribution to the demise of my marriage solidify, I am compelled to ask myself, What needs to change for me to have a richer, more realistic, more lasting relationship in the future? And the answer that keeps coming to mind is...everything. The entire structure of how I perceive relationships and their purpose in my life requires an absolute overhaul. Complete and total annihilation of previously held beliefs so that something new can be born.

In a parallel that is both sublime and ridiculous, right now, my garden looks like 1942 Berlin. I've lost two major trees to age and rot; my ancient, iconic trumpet vine when the west fence fell in a storm; the entire west side of the garden to the same fence collapse; half my cherry laurel screening hedge from a sudden hard freeze; all fifty-plus Knockout rosebushes, which comprised the foundation of my garden to rose rosette disease; half my dogwoods to the ongoing drought and subsequent water restrictions; my most recent failed *C. japonica*; and at least 30 percent of the rest of my garden simply from the changes in sun exposure due to the above-described collective catastrophes. So little of my garden is salvageable that frankly it's not worth trying. Basically, my garden is shot. Or a more poetic view could be that perhaps my garden is letting go. Complete and total annihilation so that here, too, something new can be born. A new garden, a new life, and a new understanding of relationships and love that resonates with the Me that is emerging.

In *The Prophet*, Kahlil Gibran writes:

Let there be spaces in your togetherness, And let the winds of the heavens dance between you. Love one another but make not a bond of love: Let it rather be a moving sea between the shores of your souls. Fill each other's cup but drink not from one cup. Give one another of your bread but eat not from the same loaf. Sing and dance together and be joyous, but let each one of you be alone, Even as the strings of a lute are alone though they quiver with the same music. Give your hearts, but not into each other's keeping. For only the hand of Life can contain your hearts. And stand together, yet not too near together: For the pillars of the temple stand apart, And the oak tree and the cypress grow not in each other's shadow.

Someone gave me that book for my high school graduation. I wish I had read it sooner. Not that it probably would have mattered. My idea of love at the time was better described as fusion. You know—the kind of reaction that fuels the sun. And hydrogen bombs.

I have decided that one day, if this protracted separation ever ends and Dan and I finally get divorced, whether I get to keep my house and my garden or not, I am going to plan some kind of ritual of release. I will honor what has been, what is, and what is yet to come in my life. I plan to go into my garden and remove every tainted, diseased, broken, sickly, unhealthy, ill-suited plant, and I am starting over. I shall clear away that which has already died in spirit or in fact. I shall, with purpose and conscious intention, eradicate the symbols in my garden of a belief structure that did not have fortitude to survive, but served a sacred purpose in my soul's growth and does have the wisdom to learn and do better next time. There is too much to burn everything I intend to remove, but I will have a symbolic fire in the garden. A pyre. A ceremonial release of the soul of my garden and the pain of my past. And, in turn, a metaphorical opening of the heart, mind, and spirit of my future.

Total annihilation. Release. Rebirth.

The Still Small Voice

For some reason I always seem to have trouble getting out of the house, especially if I'm going out of town, but sometimes even when I am going to the grocery store. No matter how much advance planning I do when I travel, when the time comes to walk out the door, I am nervous, stressed, and sure I've forgotten something. I go back into the house a dozen times, checking the lights, checking the cats' food, checking the sprinkler system, and on and on.

In addition to my regularly scheduled travel freak-out, this year I had been working hard at building Whimsical Gardens into a business that could reliably support me, and although I was still very fearful about that, I wanted and needed to do it so I could eventually get divorced and truly move on with my life. But ending a decades-long marriage is not something to be taken lightly, even though we had already been separated for several years. As much as part of me wanted to be free, divorce pulled at my sense of commitment. It challenged my belief in myself. I was still afraid of whether or not I could take care of myself, even though getting divorced did seem like the best way for me to care for myself now. It was something that needed to be done, but the inevitable contention that would come from this process worried me. We had begun discussing the division of assets, and I was surprised to find significantly more conflict than I had anticipated, and wondered if we were going to need to hand it over to legal experts. My mind was on the dissolution of my marriage and my thoughts around keeping it as civil a process as possible, so I was not fully present with the packing at hand, and getting out of town was even more trouble than usual.

So there I was, rushing around acting like some scattered, distracted twit who had never been out of the neighborhood before in her life, trying to leave the house and get over to where my crew was already working on a major installation at a large ranch about an hour away. Mind you, it was Fort Worth I was heading to, not some third world country. If I forgot something, I could actually buy it there. And even if I couldn't, it was only an hour away for goodness' sake! Nevertheless, trying to get out the door for this excursion was a lot harder than it should have been.

Finally, a cool two and a half hours after I was supposed to arrive in Fort Worth, I managed to get into the car with all my drafting supplies, all my files, my laptop, the drawings, all my clothes for a week, all my high-nutrition supplements I need during hot summer installations, and whatever else I thought I couldn't live without for six days. I was in the car, and I was ready to go.

Before I could hit the ignition, I had a strong feeling I needed to go back to the house.

"Ugh," I thought. "*No!* I have everything I need."

I turned on the car.

"Go back. You need to go back to the house."

"Don't be ridiculous," I told myself. "You do this *way* too much!"

I opened the garage door.

"You need to go back to the house." The feeling was louder now and very clear.

"Stop it. You're a lunatic!"

I backed out of the garage.

"You need to go back to the house."

"This is pathological."

I stopped just outside the garage and scanned my memory for anything I might have forgotten. I was sure I had everything I needed. I stepped on the accelerator to continue backing up.

"You need to go back to the house."

I put the car in park and sat there for a moment, exasperated but resigned, then got out of the car. Apparently, I needed to go back to the house. I went through the garage and down the breezeway. As I approached the back door, I noticed the tall blue bin I use for recycling that sits just outside my kitchen door. The same kitchen door, mind you, that I had just dashed back and forth past at least eleven times in the last two and a half hours.

"That's odd," I thought as I noticed there was no blue bag in the bin. "There's always a blue bag in the recycling bin."

I approached the bin and leaned over to peek inside, unsure of what I was looking for, but thinking I should just check. I stared down into the bin, and there, curled up in the corner of the bottom of the bin, on top of the wadded up blue recycling bag, was a small baby opossum.

"Oh my goodness, darling!" I exclaimed. "How in the world did you get in there?!"

He looked up at me, obviously exhausted, and very, very weakly gave me the tiniest, most unconvincing little hiss that ever happened in the world.

"Baby..."

He didn't move. He just looked at me. He didn't seem scared. He didn't try to move away. He just looked up at me with sweet little beady black eyes. I scanned the area and saw there was a box next to the tall bin that he must have climbed onto and managed to get inside, but he wasn't big enough to be able to get back out. Thank goodness the plastic bag had crumpled up under him and he had not gotten caught inside it.

I gently lifted the bin and took it over into the garden and onto the grass by a flowering silver sage. I carefully laid the bin onto its side, thinking he would crawl out, but he just sat there, so after a while I very slowly tilted it forward, and the little fellow slid out onto the grass.

He stopped, blinked in the sun for a moment, then turned around and held my gaze for a long while. He looked at me with what I would like to anthropomorphize as appreciation, but was probably just interest, and then he trotted away. I don't know how long he had been in there, but I am pretty sure if I had left town for a week, by the time I got home he would have died in the August heat from dehydration.

I've read some cultures teach that opossum comes to protect one's receptive, nurturing feminine energy. Opossum's guidance shows up when we are struggling to understand our own emotions, particularly in the area of relationships. (Seriously, you can't make this stuff up.) Because of their nocturnal nature, opossum are associated with the moon, which is also feminine energy. When offered opossum's guidance, we are aligned with all wisdom, especially the wisdom of the warrior. Not to be confused with one who rushes into rash conflict, the wise warrior has discernment, using patience, thought, strategy, and preparation to choose when to fight and when to lie still and let the storm pass. Opossum's guidance reminds us that the mind is a warrior's mightiest weapon.

And tiny, defenseless baby opossum? Well, I'm going to say that my wise warrior is just being birthed, and that I am both its embodiment and its protector.

As I returned to my car and backed out of my driveway, I thought about my fuzzy little spirit guide and his message. Any questions I might have had about how to handle the division of assets when the time comes to divorce, and when or whether to hand things over to professionals suddenly felt quietly yet firmly clear. I will choose my battles carefully because a peaceful relationship transition with my son's father is important to all of us.

And I need to trust my intuition.

Geraldine

The first time I encountered Geraldine, she was a little shy. More than a little, to be honest. She actually ran away. I was a bit disappointed by that, but her reticence didn't last. I saw her the next day in the apple orchard across from my cottage. She was about thirty feet away from me. I didn't want to spook her again, so I stayed on my cottage stoop and watched her grazing. She was beautiful. A young mule doe, tall and lean, with big brown eyes and ears that flipped forward and back, keeping tabs on her surroundings while she munched. I spoke to her very softly. So softly, in fact, I wasn't sure she could hear me, given her distance. But each time I would address her, those ears flipped forward and she lifted her head just enough to reassure herself of my exact location, then dropped it back down to return to her after-noon snacking.

She moved slowly and gracefully through the tall, clover-filled grass, not oblivious to me, but not startled like yesterday. As she followed the tastiest green shoots, still moist from the monsoon rains an hour ago, I wondered if she realized she was moving closer and closer to me with each silent, delicate step she took. I didn't move, but con-tinued to speak to her quietly, and it made me smile each time her ears would flip forward, as if to listen to me more closely. I called her Geraldine. I'm not sure why, but every time I did, she flipped her ears. After a while my soft spo-ken words caught a melody on the breeze and evolved into "The Ballad of Geraldine" by Donovan.

I sat on my front porch writing, admiring, and singing to Geraldine for a good long while, then retired to my cot-tage for a nap. The energy when I travel to Sedona, Arizona, makes me sleepy, and I have been napping a lot since I ar-rived. I've been on the toddler sleeping schedule—wake up, eat breakfast; take a morning nap; wake up, eat lunch; take an afternoon nap; wake up, eat dinner; let the stars and the crickets tell me a bedtime story, then tuck myself in for the night, with some writing and hiking here and there.

"The Ballad of Geraldine" always reminds me of Daniel, as did all songs by Donovan. In the years when we were dating and the early years of our marriage, he would play guitar and sing, always lyrical ballads and poetry in song by artists from the 1960s and '70s. I was unfamiliar with many of them, so for me they became his songs. He loved the Byrds, and folk artists like Bob Dylan, Donovan, and Dallas hometown favorite Willis Alan Ramsey. I will never forget the first time I heard Daniel play and sing. We had spent the day out and about in his MGB convertible, when he pulled into the parking lot of a guitar store. He said he wanted to browse around. Looking over the acoustic guitars, he picked a Martin with elaborate abalone inlay and took it into the rehearsal room. Having no idea what was about to come, I remember thinking, "Why are we doing this...?" He sat down, strummed a few bars, then began to play "Angel Eyes." I was floored. Daniel had a beautiful voice and played so soulfully. I later learned he had other friends who were also accomplished musicians, but none of them played with the depth of emotion that Daniel did. He was emotionally reserved in everyday life, but when he sang, his heart was fully engaged, and all the emotion I knew he must feel inside poured out through his voice and his guitar. Many of the most romantic things he ever said to me, he said through the songs of these artists. If ever we had "a song" (which we definitely didn't because he would never), it would have been Ramsey's "Angel Eyes." He never looked away from me when he sang it, and it always made me cry. I loved to listen to Daniel play and sing, but he gave it up soon after we married, frustrated by what he perceived as his lack of proficiency as the time and opportunity to rehearse dropped further and further away between his law practice and life. I encouraged him to push through the forgetfulness of his fingers and remind them by playing the songs he loved, but his perfectionism wouldn't allow it. It felt like a loss to me, but I know it was a much greater loss for him. To this day, even with all that has transpired, I can't listen to "Angel Eyes" without crying.

On the third day of my encounters with Geraldine, an amazing thing happened. I had gone up to the lodge for tea, and when I returned through the apple grove to my cottage, she was grazing very near my door. I stopped as soon as I saw her, not wanting to startle or scare her away. She glanced up at me, chewing a mouthful of grass; then after a long stare-down, she dropped her head and continued eating.

"All righty then. No big deal," I thought, and walked on over to my cottage. As I passed her, she was no more than ten feet away from me. Once inside, I got my book and my laptop, and weighed the relative chances of managing to go back outside and sit on the chaise in the tall grass Geraldine was munching without spooking her. I decided to take my chances and stepped out the cottage door.

Over the course of the next few minutes, I approached Geraldine, who was barely five feet from my chaise. She seemed cool with my proximity, so I reached for the chaise and pulled it over into the shade. I put my laptop and book on it, went back inside the cottage to get some water, then returned, sat down, and got comfy. She acted like we did this every day. She grazed as I perused the internet, periodically reading little snippets of news to her out loud as if we were some old couple who had been married for fifty years. Geraldine and I spent a good part of the day together doing our respective things, kind of ignoring each other, but truthfully, she was ignoring me more than I was ignoring her, because I was fascinated. Fascinated by her beauty, fascinated by her grace, fascinated by her intuitive clarity that I was no threat to her, fascinated by her obvious power housed in such a gentle package. I was close enough to her to see details I had only seen in photographs or heartbreaking taxidermies, which I could never bear to look at very closely. Details of her coat, her ears, her snout, even her eyelashes, her musculature, and her movements. Her ears had some pretty serious notches in them, and I wondered when and with whom she had tussled. Geraldine seemed fine with my curiosity and didn't mind that I stared.

I had to change cottages the next day since I had chosen to extend my stay by almost a week and my original cottage was not available. My new cottage was darling, but it was far removed from the orchard and the wild edges of the property where Geraldine lived, and I didn't see her again while I was there, but I was grateful for the time we spent together and the energy we shared.

Reflecting on my increasingly close encounters with Geraldine over three consecutive days as I sat in this sacred, native land surrounded by the towering red rocks of Arizona, I thought about what deer symbolize in some ancient cultures. Among other things, she is power and grace.

Power and grace—those two things rarely come together in my world. Whenever I think about power and grace, I think about watching Glenn ice skate. He always wanted to stay right by my side the only time we skated together, but I was obviously holding him back, so when I insisted he release himself from babysitting me with my utter lack of ice skating proficiency, he finally took off, moving fast across the ice. I loved to watch him skate. When he was ice skating, he was the most beautiful, fluid, dynamic expression of power and grace I had ever seen. When Glenn skated, he embodied freedom.

Power and grace—I had witnessed Daniel managing potentially confrontational professional debates with a calm intelligence and quiet but palpable authority that never ceased to amaze me. I, on the other hand, never seemed to manage both at the same time. I had either power *or* grace, and often neither. More often than not, I had given my power away or never knew it was there in the first place. And when I could dredge up enough anger or frustration to try to assert it, oy...it was awkward. That old pendulum of powerlessness was constantly swinging too far the other way, and my attempts at standing up for myself usually came out rather badly. Very discouraging. Often embarrassing. Sometimes humiliating. But I've been working on it. Working on all of it. The power, the grace, and the integration of those two things in my life.

Deer, and especially does, also represent gentleness with self and others. Here again, I score in the bottom half. Not with others—I can be pretty good at that, but when it comes to being gentle with myself, or requiring others to be gentle with me, I think it's fair to say I have been an abject failure. Historically, that is. But I've been trying to improve that, too. Not long ago, I was beginning an interesting new therapy called Network chiropractic. It's called "chiropractic," but it is nothing like the pop and crack bodywork most people think of when they hear that word. I would describe Network as being more like energy work. I went to an information session and learned that Network treats the nervous system to help process trauma held in the body. Given my history, I knew I needed to give it a try. The touch is so gentle it is frequently almost indiscernible, which, as much as I wanted this process to be successful, triggered my skepticism. Lying facedown on the table at my second or third session, as Dr. Tyler Lewis barely touched points on my spine and released, I set my teeth, mentally rolled my eyes, and thought, "Seriously? You think that's doing anything? I can barely even feel that." And then suddenly, an emotion rose to my consciousness that said, "What if everyone had always treated you this gently?" And I broke into deep, anguished tears.

That was a turning point for me. A whole new way of seeing the world. A world not only where I was loving to others, but where I could fairly and reasonably expect them to be loving to me. A world where I could—and indeed must—treat myself with the same love, care, and kindness I give, if I am ever to receive it fully from anyone else. It hasn't been easy. Old habits can be brutal. I would never speak to anyone else the way I regularly speak to myself. But my awareness is higher now, and each time I hear myself say something to or about myself that is cutting and cruel, I interrupt that behavior with the same power and absolute shutdown I would have used if anyone had ever dared speak to my son that way when he was little. And then I apologize. I apologize to me. It's the least I can do after being so mean. And the next time, I try to be kinder to myself.

My three increasingly intimate encounters with Geraldine on three consecutive days opened my heart a bit wider. Her gifts of power, grace, and gentleness guided me to a deeper awareness of places where I still have significant room to grow and expand my capacity for love, particularly with myself. Many sacred gifts come in groups of three, and today I am reminded: "Now abideth faith, hope, and love, these three. But the greatest of these is love."

Chapter 3

Germination

Invincible Summer

Winter's soft, gray stillness has fallen, and the garden sleeps. I call it the Zen period of the garden, when the ground and I are contemplative, and everything is pure potential.

During the years my family lived in Scotland when I was a little girl, winter meant darkness. With only about six hours of daylight in the deep winter months, I became accustomed to going to school in the dark and coming home in the dark for months on end. Because of this, I grew to be very comfortable in both the presence and the energy of darkness. It's a good thing. As things turned out, I would spend a great deal of time in the darkest recesses of my psyche before I would begin to uncover that for which my soul ached.

But when the dark night of the soul passes months, and

stretches into years, how can we know if it will ever lift? When the anguish of our existential pain is so deep and so prolonged that we begin to forget what its absence feels like, how do we know if we will even recognize the other side of it if we get there? Albert Camus wrote, "When the soul suffers too much it develops a taste for misfortune." Now that's a scary thought. Scary because I know it can be true. I have spent a lot of time with people who are spiritual seekers and people who are on a path of self-discovery and awareness. During this time, I have been in the company of many who have experienced unimaginable tragedy, abuse, loss, addiction, or other profound unhappiness. And I have witnessed most of them, at least for a while, self-perpetuate the feelings associated with their trauma by subconsciously seeking people or events that will either mimic or actually re-create those same visceral experiences. I know this happens, and it's hard to watch from the helpless sidelines of friendship. And what I *really* know is that I do not want to do this to myself. I mean...I don't want to do it anymore. I am pretty sure I have done it in the past. The fairly recent past, if I'm honest. I'm not sure how often I've done it, or for how long. But I am absolutely certain I do not want to do it anymore. Yet how do we stop doing something when we are not even aware we are doing it? How do we override deep, established neural pathways that seek familiar ground, perceiving it as safe, even if that very ground is painful, unhealthy, and perhaps even dangerous?

Over the course of my life, I have had to deal with significant trauma, tragedy, and loss. There was nothing I could do about those things. They happened, and they shaped me into who I am. But I'm tired of always feeling slightly tragic. And I'm tired of being afraid that everyone I love will abandon or betray me, or both. It is not my nature to be sad. Just as it is not of nature to be sad. Nature is exuberant, vibrant, and unrestrained. Nature doesn't question the motives of its circumstances. Trees do not wonder what they might have done to create this harsh winter or that summer of drought. They adapt or they die. Period. And if they are able to adapt, they simply carry on. They do not wallow in an endless stream of self-recrimination or existential angst, perpetuating their own suffering by running an internal obstacle course designed for failure, conducted by the unanswerable "Why?" Nor do they engage in an exhaustive analysis of what they might have done to attract these painful conditions into their lives—an exercise in metaphysical malpractice.

Of course, we are not trees. But the question of when this analysis ceases to be helpful or productive bears consideration. For those who are on a path of expansion and self-understanding, it is divine discontent that drives us, so I am not suggesting that we throw all that away or ignore our hard-earned knowledge and wisdom. I would simply like to have a grasp of when it is time to just let go and move on. And when I have the answer to that, I'd love to get the large print, bold type, paint-by-numbers, step-by-step instruction book for dummies on exactly how to do it.

People tell me I am strong, and maybe I am, though I don't feel particularly strong most of the time. But like

Camus, I know that there is "within me, an invincible summer." An intractable optimism. A defiant demand to the Universe that I will not only survive, I will thrive. A burning insistence on joy deep within me that refuses to be extinguished. And it is that which gives me the courage to carry on.

Dark Luna

Tonight there was a much anticipated total lunar eclipse. At least it was much anticipated if you go by the number of column inches it was taking up in my social media newsfeeds. Everybody from *Earth & Sky*, Space.com, and NASA to shamans and astrologers was talking about the total eclipse of the supermoon, or the lunar perigee, as the space pros call it. How long since the last one (1988), how long until the next one (2033), what it meant according to the stars (be alert for things that are hidden), what it heralded (the end of the world . . . again), and on and on.

Even nightclubs (serving SuperMoonshine tonight only!) and foodies (MoonPies, Milky Ways, Mars bars, and anything made of cheese) were cashing in on the Super Big Blood Moon Eclipse Event.

Over the course of my life, I have dragged myself out of my toasty bed in the wee hours of the morning to experience lunar eclipses a few times before. I was underwhelmed. Yep, the moon looks like it's turning kind of reddish. Big whoop. It's a very slow process, and frankly, I was never that interested or sufficiently captivated to stay awake long enough to watch the whole thing. I was sleepy. If I'm going to wake up in the middle of the night and go out into the freezing cold, it better be for a really good reason. Like a fire alarm. Lunar eclipses just never quite had the requisite oomph, so I always ended up going back to bed before it was over, with a resounding sense of "meh."

That said, my assessment of lunar eclipses as being much ado about nothing was, to be fair, not based on ever having actually seen one. Not really. Not completely. How often do we do that? Make a judgment based on limited knowledge or experience. Or based on *no* personal knowledge or experience at all, just someone else's word. Or based on fear. That happens a lot. Or worse, based on *someone else's* fear that got transferred to us subtly or overtly, and lodged in our minds as true, even though we really have no idea if it actually *is* true or not.

Having this vague sense that I actually didn't know what a lunar eclipse was really like, I decided to try again. Fortunately this year, the very accommodating and much lauded supermoon had planned its eclipse party at a reasonable hour in my neck of the woods, right around ten p.m., so waking in the wee hours wasn't going to be a problem. That, together with the cooperation of a warm, clear night, was enough to get me to drive over to the parking lot of a nearby vacant shopping center. It had no trees, no people, no lights, and an unobstructed view of the sky. I brought a nice bottle of wine, some dolmas and hummus with pita chips, and set out to see what all the fuss was about.

By the time I got to the parking lot and drove around to find the best view, the moon had cleared the treetops of the neighborhood across the street. It was the moon of my childhood. Clear, flat, and bright blue-white. Not what I would call "super," but definitely bigger than usual and beautiful as always. She was the moon I often spoke to from my hot tub when I felt lost, afraid, or filled with longing. She was the moon I sometimes turned to in frustration—the Saint Genevieve to my Guinevere. I knew this moon. We were old friends.

I opened my wine, pulled out my little picnic, turned on my Ludovico Einaudi playlist, and waited.

Before long, the mass of the earth began to interrupt the light of the sun, and a small edge of the moon fell into shadow. I sat in my car observing the process as the slow creep of darkness overtook her light. Once she was half covered, I felt a twinge, a need to open my window, as if it were somehow impeding my view. By the time she was two-thirds veiled, I turned off the music. When she was seven-eighths covered, I had to get out of my car. I stood alone in the darkness and watched the moon's reflected light disappear. As shadow covered her, it also fell across the land, and the night became darker. Then, as if a stage light had been flipped on from the wings of the cosmos, the moon popped from a flat, two-dimensional, blue-white object into a surreal three-dimensional terracotta ball in the sky. Looking more like a fanciful computer artist's vision of the sky over a far-off planet, or a child's model of Mars, this unfamiliar orb seemed close enough to bat at, like a red moon piñata. I knew the moon was a sphere, but I had never focused on the fact that, despite what my intellect knew, what my eyes had always seen was a disk. But now there was no mistaking it was a sphere. Newly visible highlights and shadings revealed contours and craters. I could see volume, dimension, complexity, and I realized how much there was I didn't know about my old friend.

Staring up at this alien russet sphere, I considered how fiercely we fight for the light. How furiously we defend against darkness. But what I saw tonight was not light versus darkness. It was a teaser. An amuse-bouche. An invitation to come closer, to look deeper, to seek treasures heretofore unnoticed. It was a reminder that there are hidden truths which can only be found when we allow ourselves to look again at the most familiar things in our lives through a different lens. I understand now why they call the period when the moon is completely in shadow its totality, because what I saw tonight was wholeness, and it was more beautiful than I could have imagined.

I have spent a lot of years working with facilitators to help guide me with relatively safe passage into my own darkness. What I have learned is that the Shadow aspects of my life are what give me depth, complexity, and inspiration. It is the Shadow which gives us dimension. When we doggedly insist on pure light at the expense of the Shadow, we remain two-dimensional. Shiny, bright, cheery, but flat. To deny the Shadow is to deny our totality—our wholeness. For all our celebration of light, it was during a total eclipse that the moon suddenly became vastly more interesting and compelling. Luna's normal vivid whiteness happens when the sun's light is reflected so brightly that the moon's features are flashed out into obscurity. How often does this happen to the feminine? Young girls are frequently overshadowed by the dynamic, more confident energy of boys. Women are often spoken over, and we tend to allow ourselves to be hushed rather than appear rude. We are expected to be bright, attractive, appealing, friendly, charming, and especially, nice. But all this accommodation frequently comes at the expense of our honesty, our depth, our complexity, our voice. The richness of our range. Authenticity is a high price to pay for being pleasant.

I was taught that my highest and best use was as a wife and a mother. To stand demurely reflecting the light of another, like a good girl. But is that really my highest and best use? Even though some of my happiest years were as a stay-at-home mother, and I firmly believe motherhood is one of the most important jobs in the world, was that it? Was my only option now to find another man whose light I could amplify or reflect?

On an average night, Luna's details, her textures, the fullness of her form are washed out by the sun's glaring light. But every so often, Mother Earth positions herself between the sun and the moon, offering Luna a respite. An hour or so of full expression. Time to be as big and showy and multidimensional and complicated and rich and fascinating as she truly is. In poetic irony, it is when Luna is in shadow that she is finally no longer being overshadowed.

How subtle and graceful the Universe is.

It Came to Pass

The garden has been one of my greatest teachers, and like any great teacher, when I do not fully grasp a subject, she explains it differently, again and again, until I understand. Some of the lessons I understand immediately. Others are more of a challenge. One such challenging lesson for me is that of letting go, and for that there is no more basic teacher than flowers. Few things are lovelier and even fewer more fleeting. Truly, one cannot be a gardener without some ability to accept death and loss.

When I did a lot of competitive floral design (as weird as that sounds), people would often say to me, "Isn't it a shame that so much effort went into making such beauty that will only last a few days?" My stock answer was "Part of the beauty of floral design is its ephemeral nature. It is beauty for beauty's sake. It cannot be possessed."

I talk a good game. While that may sound all profound and philosophical and detached, the truth is that anyone who knows me well knows that I can cling to people and things I care about like Velcro on steroids. So is it any wonder that I spend every day working and dealing with flowers? Some of the most beautiful yet most impermanent materials in the world. It's almost as if the Universe is saying, "Okay, Miss Attachments-Are-Us, let's practice. Here is something beautiful. Work with it. Commit to it. Love it. Now...let it go." And again. Nature has had me on the lather, rinse, repeat cycle for decades.

Of course, the daily fading of flowers in the garden is hardly a gut-wrenching experience. Not only because there are so many, but because we know that there are always more where those came from. We absolutely know this about flowers, yet how do we translate that faith into other aspects of our lives? How can we look at the steady, seemingly infinite flow and rotation of blossoms in the garden and trust that the void we feel when a person or relationship transitions out of our lives will be refilled by a beautiful new one? It won't be the same, of course, but it can be magnificent, rich, and fulfilling in its own right. Better even than the ongoing heartbreak we clung to for so long. It may be irises that are fading, and roses that are beginning to bloom, but both are stunning, and sometimes, we need to release the iris so we can be fully present and appreciate the rose. It's like trying to enjoy dessert while you are still eating dinner. You can't completely enjoy one while you are still wrapped up in the other.

The answer to this existential question came to me subtly (for once) while I was at a Christmas Eve service and a Bible story was being read. It began, "And so it came to pass..." After hearing that phrase countless times from hundreds of Bible stories over the course of my life, I suddenly heard it completely anew, and realized what it meant. "It came *to pass*." All things come *to pass*. They do not come to stay.

There it was, right there, in the opening line of over four hundred parables and stories in the Bible, reassurance that all things pass. No matter the accompanying worry, fear, trauma, or crisis, everything comes *to pass*. It is *an* experience, but it is not *the* experience. Our lives are a series of ups and downs, loves and losses, victories and defeats, successes and failures, acceptances and rejections. And all of them—the so-called good and the so-called bad—they all come to pass. Nothing is forever, except the eternal nature of change. Our job is to open ourselves to receive each new person and experience, find its meaning, embrace its gifts, then release it, making way for a new relationship, a new love, a new experience, a new life to emerge.

Into our gardens and into our lives, all things come to pass.

Fall Blooming
Flowers

Throughout time, the reemergence of flowers in the spring has been a symbol of the rebirth and renewal of life. In many early civilizations it was considered both a symbol and a source of divinity, and it's easy to see why. It is nearly impossible to look at the tender green shoots and gentle buds of spring as they push their way out after months of bitter cold, snow, and dormancy that resembles death without a feeling of comfort, appreciation, relief, and a sense of the holy. Yes, spring flowers are a universal symbol of renewal, but this year I have been especially touched by something else in my garden: fall blooming flowers.

I have always been the kind of girl who was drawn to the unusual and unexpected. Being different and unique has been a driving force in my artistic and personal endeavors for as long as I can remember. The idea of fitting in with the crowd is absolutely anathema to me. When people comment on how I think out of the box, I always say, "What box?" and I'm only kidding some of the time. So maybe that is part of why I love fall blooming flowers. The simple fact that they don't bloom when everybody else does is enough for them to delight me. But this year, their impact has not only been stronger, but has also had an added dimension I don't recall noticing before. This year, fall comes on the heels of an exceptionally difficult summer where I was facing some very dark memories. Processing through them has been profound and exhausting, but transformational. As the lessons from those experiences fully take hold and begin to integrate into the Me that is emerging, I am struck by the message of flowers that are budding and blooming in my garden this autumn.

Ever since Dan and I separated five years ago, Texas has been experiencing an extended drought, and our summers have been especially protracted. This summer in particular has seemed endless. Long, dry, and very, very hot. Fry an egg on the sidewalk hot. Park twice as far away as you need to just to park in the shade hot. Hotter than a firecracker. Hotter than a jalapeño eating contest. Hotter than hell. And I was like a method actor. Complete and utter immersion in both the internal experience of hell and its meteorological out-picturing.

So when the heat broke this year, both actually and metaphorically, and fall touched my shoulder with the sweet breath of relief, and a whole range of flowers began to bud and bloom in my garden, I saw them differently than I had seen them before. These were not spring's tender, sweet babes, emerging into soft, easy, warm days after winter's chilly sleep. They were the phoenix rising from the searing heat and ashes of the summer of my transformation, defiantly blooming with the audacious fire-be-damned determination that I felt. These flowers emerged from parched earth, punishing heat, and record-breaking drought with every bit of the splendor, grandeur, and dignity that their spring sisters display. They were new, yes, and they were still flowers with all the sensual softness any flower petal possesses, but I did not see them as fragile nor delicate in any way. These were powerful flowers, flush with the vigor and strength of a survivor.

I will always love spring flowers and the tenderness of their message. But fall flowers—now there's something I can identify with.

Just Passing Through

It was a beautiful fall morning and I was up early. Not for any particular reason, except that when I first awoke, the shimmering light of the day poured through my windows and beckoned me into it. I walked downstairs, and when I opened the front door, it was like stepping into Oz. The sky was golden, pink, and orange, and the three giant American elm trees in my front yard were at the peak of their autumn show in a cadmium yellow so clear and bright it's hard to believe it occurs in nature. With branches still full and shimmering, the trees had dropped enough leaves overnight to cover the ground with a solid yellow carpet that sparkled from a light frost, all made more vivid and luminous by dawn's golden light. I was so overcome by the beauty of this aurulent world that I took a step out the door, and stopped to breathe in the colors.

It was then that I noticed movement out of the corner of my eye. Rather a lot of movement, on both sides. I turned my head slowly to see what could be so active against the house and what I saw was so unexpected, it took me a moment to process it. The shrubs flanking my doorway appeared to be alive with subtle but steady vibrations. I looked more closely. The foliage had virtually disappeared, leaving no visible trace of green. In its place was a visual symphony of pulsating orange, silver, and black. I squinted to give my eyes and my mind time to focus and sort out this amorphous, undulating mass where my hedges used to be.

Butterflies! The bushes were covered—solidly covered—in monarch butterflies. There were hundreds of them, thousands, maybe tens of thousands. There were so many monarchs it was impossible to see where one butterfly stopped and another began. They blanketed the entire length of the hedges on both sides of the house; fifty, maybe sixty feet of four-foot-tall hollies. They were stacked and piled and clustered beside, on top of, and underneath each other, deep into the shrubs. Though each was stationary on its spot, all of them were rapidly moving in place. I realized they were fluttering their wings to fend off the morning frost before they could continue on their long trek to Mexico for the winter.

As I watched this gathering of rare guests warm their little wings in my garden, I felt profoundly graced by their presence, and by the magnificence of the morning. I felt expansive and amazed by the limitless abundance that surrounds us, and such a bone-deep sense of gratitude for it all that I whispered, "Thank you," aloud.

At that moment, a few monarchs lifted from the hedge, floated upward, and flew away, followed by a few more, and a few more after that. And within about five minutes, they were gone. A steady stream of remarkable, tiny travelers, fluttering off and away, into the brightening southern sky.

I sank down onto the front step and remained there for a long while, not wanting the experience to be over. And as I sat, I thought about how when things go wrong, we are always reminded that tomorrow is another day, and that this too shall pass. But it is important to remember how transient the good times are as well, and how important it is to be present to the beauty of this moment, now, and be grateful. For it too shall pass, often far more quickly than we would prefer.

Revelation Revelry

It was a sparkling fall day, with air so chilly and crisp it tingled inside my nostrils. As I stepped into the hot tub and sank into the warm churning water, the contrast on my skin of hot and cold, wet and dry, was dizzying and exhilarating. I don't go out into the hot tub during the day very often, but this fresh, fabulous fall day was so beautiful, it dragged me out to join it.

My senses felt acute. I was filled with joy. The relief of waking up to such a beautiful day unburdened by the suffocating weight of an unhappy marriage felt like the most glorious experience of pure joy and freedom I could ever remember. Plunging myself into the steaming hot water, then coming back up into the sharp cold air heightened my senses more and more until I threw out my arms to the Universe and shouted my gratitude to the sky. I waved and called back to squawking geese as they passed over me heading to warmer climes, and danced and splashed in the pool like a giddy child.

Time passed without my notice in this naked, ecstatic water dance. Even when the energy of the dance began to fade, the electrical joy that surged through my body remained high. I laid my head back on the edge of the spa and allowed my body to float freely, pushed by the bubbling water. Steam rose from my skin where it had been submerged and was now exposed. I felt such gratitude, the lightness of liberation radiated all around me.

As I bobbed gently around the spa to the song of soft breezes, falling leaves, and migrating birds, a sudden cascade of thoughts slashed through my bliss. What if Daniel was right? What if Daniel was 100 percent right? What if Daniel was 100 percent right...about everything?

Once they started, these thoughts poured into me so fast, I could hardly sort them out or keep up with them. What if everything he said—every criticism, every insult, every accusation, every harsh word...was true?

I suddenly felt lifted as if an enormous invisible weight on my throat had just vaporized. Somehow, a magical new perspective had found its way through the joy door in my heart. Suddenly I could see his perspective, and through that lens, I could see why he felt the way he felt. It wasn't that he actually *was* right. Of course, all the problems in our marriage were not my fault. And no, the harsh, hurtful words were neither fair nor justified. But suddenly I could see what he saw. I could see a seed of truth. Not a giant avocado seed, but a seed nevertheless. A small seed that, like all seeds, held within it an entire universe. I found myself again in a parallel reality like the one I stepped into during my parking lot epiphany about Bon Bon and Julia. I had fallen through a perspective portal, into the universe in which Dan had been living for years. And as this universe unfurled before me, I could see kernels of truth in each of his refrains, and how they could—from a wounded perspective—support his point of view. Each accusation that had caused me such suffering was suddenly surrounded by a luminous halo, and vibrated with the light and energy of a radically new point of view. I could see how the seeds of this perspective could hold the power to grow and flourish into a fully formed sense of rightness. He wasn't exactly right, but he was not completely wrong either. Just as I suspected years ago when he first moved out—that puzzle I recognized as a paradox about how he and I could hold opposite views yet both be right—suddenly *I got it*. I understood how. We had been two people looking at the same white poplar leaf from different sides. One insisting the leaf was obviously a rich, dark green while the other angrily and indignantly scoffed that *anyone* could see it was pure white. When this revelation landed in my body, it hit like a gigantic asteroid. One where "nothing survives, not even bacteria." A global attitude killer. In that moment, all my resistance to his disparaging words vanished. Without the tension and the reactive, energetic wall of being constantly on the defensive, I could actually see his side. And with that opening, victimhood, blame, and anger gushed out. In their absence, forgiveness flowed in. It was the most liberating moment of my life.

The Littlest
Phoenix

It happened so suddenly. A loud thud just to my left. I startled and turned to see a cedar waxwing staggering, stunned on the ground just outside my door. Her flock was still fluttering in the yaupon tree a few feet away, feeding on the heavily berried branches. This little one had flown into the glass door by my chair, the only glass door or window in the house without a soft screen that prevents such calamities.

She stood beak open, taking quick, sharp, gasping breaths as I held mine. My hope was to see her calm in a few minutes and fly away, but that didn't happen. Instead, after several minutes in the same frightened, panting stance, she shifted a little, then fell over onto her side, and tears welled up in my eyes. She was still breathing, each breath sharp and panicked, and I feared for her chances. Suddenly, the flock members who were still in the yaupon lifted en masse and flew to other nearby trees. A mockingbird had swooped in to defend his food source, and the waxwings acquiesced for the moment. I worried that they would leave my little casualty alone. After all, what could they do for her? It is one of the problems with being a bird. Nothing can really be done to help a friend in need, and yet it pained me that none of them flew down to her aid.

Sitting on the other side of the glass door, I tried not to move too much lest the shadow of my form cause her more anxiety, but when that mockingbird swept down beside, I waved my arms to shoo him away. At first he hopped back a step or two, but approached her again in a potentially menacing way, so I moved closer to the glass and waved more aggressively, and he flew off. A part of me was sorry to send off the only bird who had come to see about her, but mockingbirds can be mean, and I didn't want to risk him pecking at her when she was so vulnerable.

Her flock hung around nibbling on the yaupon periodically, but after a while they left. When they did, I felt a tug in my heart. Did she feel them leave her? Did she know they had left? Would they come back for her? What if she recovered tonight? Would she be able to find them? All these questions swirled through my mind as I debated whether or not to go out to her myself. A part of me felt I should stay away and let nature take its course, but another part wanted to go to her, hold her, let her feel my warmth and care.

I decided to go outside.

Once there, I could see a few of her flock in trees nearby and felt grateful they had not all left her. I walked around to the side where she lay and spoke softly to her, but once near, I could see two dark, wet pools the size of my thumbnail, plus several small ones on the other side. It looked like a lot of blood for a little bird to lose. I couldn't see any external lesions, which probably meant internal injuries, but I'm not really sure which is worse. I reached down and very gently stroked her. At first she didn't move, but then she lifted her head and looked at me. I slowly caressed her little head, and she laid it back down. I wanted to hold her, but was afraid to overstep her trust or worsen her unseen wounds. So I just knelt next to her, stroking her slowly and very gently as I cried. I didn't want her to die, but I knew it wasn't my decision.

After a while, she closed her beak. Her heaving breaths continuing, but softer than the desperate panting. While I was with her, the rest of her flock flew off, maybe because she was being taken care of, but more likely because they were afraid of me. I'm not sure how long I stayed with her, murmuring soft words of compassion, surrounding her with light, and occasionally touching her ever so lightly. In time, I decided to leave her to her own healing if it was to come, hoping her friends would return and watch over her from the treetops nearby. I had recently read an *Audubon* article saying that contrary to our past understanding, birds can smell, so I plucked a small, fragrant cluster of blossoms from the nearby sweet olive *Osmanthus*, laid it next to her, then went back into the house.

Cedar waxwings have been one of my favorite birds ever since I first discovered them in my garden when we moved back to the Park Cities as my son was approaching school age. I had turned one of the upstairs bedrooms into my painting studio because it overlooked the garden. One day, when all three windows were thrown open to invite in the crisp spring air, the tall variegated privet tree outside the window abruptly surged to life with the rapid beat of countless wings. With no screens on my windows, and the treetop within arm's reach, out of nowhere, an entire flock of birds was practically right inside my studio. I put down my paintbrush and moved as close as I could to the windows to watch, but staggered back when the pulse of their wings synchronized to a deep rhythmic beat and all forty or fifty birds lifted from the tree as one and flew to the telephone wires along the alley. As they did, a similar group cycled from the wires to the tree and began to feed on its heavily berried branches. Glancing back and forth between the telephone wires, the surrounding treetops, and my berrying tree, I counted four, maybe five groups of these birds, who by all appearances were systematically sharing the berries on my privet tree. Fascinating! Furthermore, I was captivated by the beauty of these birds. A little smaller than a cardinal with a similar crest on their heads, these were elegant birds in both form and color. Bodies of seamless, muted shades of cream and taupe melt into gray on their wings. Each had a dramatic black eye mask and a very pale, butter-yellow breast. These soft neutral shades were offset by wings with wildly vivid red tips, and the tidy, squared-off ends of their tail feathers were bright cadmium yellow. As this was pre-internet days, I dashed downstairs to find my bird identification book and looked them up.

What I read solidified my new love for these exquisite birds. Very social, flocking birds, cedar waxwings are rarely seen alone and are famous for the care they take to ensure the entire flock is equally well fed. In addition to the feeding rotations I had witnessed, cedar waxwings have been observed passing a single berry down a line of birds on a wire, so each one gets a bite. The sharing of fruit is so integral to this species, it is even a part of their mating ritual. The male brings a berry to the female, she takes it, then passes it back to him. Back and forth they share, until she accepts both him and his berry, and their union is sealed.

Watching this beautiful creature lie still and injured on the ground before me, having crashed against a solid glass door she did not expect to encounter and could not see, I couldn't help but think about how often I have slammed up against my own glass ceiling only to find myself prostrate, stunned, and metaphorically bleeding from the injuries of my self-doubt. I felt a deep compassion for that little bird, not just because of her experience, but because she reminded me of myself. I didn't just want her to survive. At some deep, personal level I needed her to.

I had things to do that day, but I didn't want to leave her. I readjusted my chair so she was in my direct line of sight. I read and made a few phone calls while I watched her. Her breathing stabilized, and once she even lifted her head and looked around, but then lay back down again and

was mostly still. About an hour and a half later she began to shift—a twitch here, a shiver there, then with one
sudden movement, she pulled herself up into a standing position. Upright and hunkered into herself like a tight little
puffball, she appeared to be a young bird. Standing now,
crouched into herself, eyes mostly closed, she was breathing normally but was clearly still unsteady. I continued to
watch her as she began to move a little, then stop. She made
a tiny turn toward me, then stopped again for half an hour
or so, then a tiny turn more my way, then stopped again for
a while. Each time she would rest after her movements and
let herself adjust, closing her eyes, listening to her body.

After four or five such tiny turns, and a couple of hours,
she was facing me. She stayed in this place for a long time.
Again, she would rest her eyes and go within, then open
them and look straight at me. I spoke to her very quietly,
and though I knew she couldn't hear my voice, I hoped she
could feel my energy.

"I believe in you," I said. "You are so beautiful," I told
her. "If you are still in this place as it is getting dark, I will
bring you in to keep you safe and I'll take you to a doctor
tomorrow," I promised her. She was surrounded by my loving energy and focus. Prayer, if you will. I drifted off into
my reading, but whenever I saw her move in my peripheral
vision, I looked up at her and sent her more loving encour-
agement.

About four hours after she collided with the glass door,
she tilted her head to one side and then the other. Then she
shifted a little and looked behind her, up into the yaupon

tree where her flock had been. Her movements were coordinated and almost perky. Suddenly, she hopped around a quarter turn, looked back at me, then took off for the nearest low-hanging branch.

"You've got to be kidding me!" I exclaimed as I jumped out of my chair toward the glass door to get a better look.

She sat on that branch for another half hour or so before a scout arrived from her flock. Then another, then a few more. Within minutes the tree was filled with forty or fifty cedar waxwings fluttering from branch to branch, in a berry-eating frenzy. My little phoenix stayed still on her branch amid all the swirl around her. The first group flew off and a second group swooped in, bending the slender branches low with the weight of multiple birds. Group two fed, then flew, and another came in with their carefully choreographed shared feeding rotations. Through four sets of mini flocks, my phoenix stayed perfectly still on her branch, but when a large robin swept in, scattering the flock, to my amazement, she took off with them. I was sad that in the flurry of five dozen birds, I couldn't keep her in sight, but I watched the flock until they landed in a high, bare tree a few hundred feet away. No one fell out of the sky, so I felt sure she had been strong enough to make it all the way.

Over the course of the rest of the day, groups of cedar waxwings descended on the yaupon for a few minutes, then dashed off in unison as another group dropped in. Here and gone, here and gone again, small sections of the larger flock shared berries from my tree, then dotted the high branches of the still-barren shade trees surrounding the garden, resting and digesting before circling off to who knows where for a while, then returning for another nibble. A local mockingbird and a couple of robins continued to try to defend the food source, but the waxwings' numbers were too great. As much as I love the cedar waxwings, I can see how the locals probably perceive them as marauding herds coming through and stripping the trees of berries the local birds had rationed to last all winter. By afternoon, the waxwing numbers were far fewer, and they were sharing the tree with a cardinal, two robins, two nuthatches, a couple of sparrows, and a dark-eyed junco. I would periodically look out when the tree was still, thinking all the birds were gone, but each time I checked over the course of the day, there sat a single cedar waxwing in the yaupon, quiet and still. She remained there until nightfall.

In the morning when I awoke and drew open my curtains, the yaupon was almost completely bare. The flock had obviously been there very early because when dusk fell the night before, it still had about 30 percent of its fruit. I was glad the flock was still in the neighborhood this morning, but sorry I had missed so much of their activity, and a little sad to think they might have moved on completely since the tree was virtually stripped. But as I sat down to write, a shadow caught my eye deep within the yaupon. There she was, perched on a branch near the trunk, quiet and still. Not feeding, just resting. It was my little phoenix, conserving her strength and continuing to heal in the comfort of a place she felt safe.

I was glad to see her taking all the time she needed to

regain her strength and heal. I know how that is. Healing takes longer than we would prefer, but you can't rush it or you end up right back where you were, and sometimes worse off than before. Toward the end of the second day, I heard the familiar high-pitched whistle-like call of cedar waxwings. I looked across the garden, and high in the tree-tops along the back fence was her flock. One scout flew over and perched near her. They sat together for a time, and after a while she glided down to the spot where she had fallen the day before. She hopped around where her dried blood still lay, then looked up toward me through the window. We stared at each other for a little while. I smiled at her when she cocked her head to one side. Then she fluttered her wings, and as she lifted off the ground, her friend flew out of the yaupon to join her, and together they flew to her flock and away.

As I watched them disappear, I nodded to myself. If she can make it, so can I.

The Great Escape

Outside my bedroom door, I have a screen drape. It's like a screen door, but less effective. It hangs from a tension rod and has little Velcro tabs on each side about midway down that attach to the door frame, and is weighted at the hem to keep it from blowing around too much. All of these are good ideas, but once put into practical application, they work only marginally well. The screen gaps a little on the sides, and it's a bit too long, so it gaps at the bottom, too. And when the breeze blows with sufficient enthusiasm, the whole thing waves like a flag. Nevertheless, it works better than the aqua sparkle tulle I had hanging there before, and is certainly better than nothing.

Truth be told, I had nothing shielding my open doorways for years and loved it that way. Much of the back of my house is glass, and the six glass doors that lead out to the garden are some of my favorite things about this house. I can throw them open on pretty days and, like a portal to Narnia, suddenly the entire house becomes a part of the garden. I had never experienced many negative repercussions of this unifying of indoors and out. Yes, the occasional insect would fly in, and I did find a baby bunny in my dining room once, but for the most part, mosquitoes have never been attracted to me, so the biggest reason for screen doors didn't really apply to me, and all bunnies are welcome. There was one evening, however, when I was sitting in my living room talking on the telephone. The double glass doors were open wide, and the lights were off. As evening fell, a large bobcat sauntered over and stopped right on the threshold, looking in. That did give me pause. Mostly because I was afraid Daisy, my aging cat who was sleeping at my feet, would wake up and charge the wildcat, unaware that her alpha status did not apply in this case. But the bobcat and I came to an easy, acceptable understanding. I put down the phone and slowly stood up. As I did, she looked over and our eyes met. I calmly held her gaze, waited there a few minutes, then very gingerly took one small step toward her. After a beat, she backed up a step. I stayed in place for a moment, then took another step toward her, and she backed up a few steps. We did this little dance for about eight or ten minutes, until I was at the outer edge of the covered porch and she was at the far edge of the pool. Then she finally turned and padded off, deep into the garden, and everything was fine.

All this harmony with nature was well and good until one morning, around ten o'clock, when I heard Daisy do that scary cat "ya wanna fight?!" yowl-scream. I ran into the living room to find her crouched on the threshold of the double glass doors, all six and a half pounds of her, puffed up, ears flat, with her meanest arched-back "I can take you" stance, facing off a bobcat kitten who was shorter than Daisy, but clearly outweighed her by double. I shouted to Daisy and as they flew apart, the bobcat kitten ran, but it was young and little enough that I knew for a fact that her mama was not far off, and lovely though they are in the garden and the woods, I did not want a protective bobcat mother in my living room thinking she needed to defend her kitten from me or from Daisy. That day I decided something had to change. It was time to get a barrier of some sort, but I was so reluctant to diminish my view of the garden, I just could not bring myself to get screen doors. So, after much consideration and consternation, I settled on screen drapes, mostly because they were easily removable.

As it turns out, the one I leave up pretty much all the time is on my bedroom door that faces north. It is here that I sit most often. This is where I contemplate, where I talk on the phone, where I work if I am using my laptop, and where I write. My big brown chair is positioned such that when the door is open, the breeze comes directly across me with its soft embrace, and I can smell the sweet olive *Osmanthus* when it is blooming. Since we have a lot of open-door days in Texas, this screen drape became something of a permanent fixture that I rarely noticed anymore. Until late last summer.

I was sitting as I do, in my big brown chair, when I noticed an orb weaver on the inside of the screen drape. It was a spider of noticeable size. She wasn't doing much. Just hanging around waiting for some hapless bug who was lower on the food chain to offer himself up as dinner. She held my attention for a while, as much because of her size as anything, but then soon enough, I went back to my business. The next day, she was still there. And the next, and the next. Apparently, she had taken up residence on the inside of the screen. I confess I worried a little that she couldn't find her way back out, but enough ants and other bugs were wandering in that she was thriving and growing, so I didn't worry about her too much. I did think about her, though. I thought about how much happier she might be stationed, for example, in a rosebush or perhaps in a crape myrtle. Somewhere she could feel the warm sun. A place that drew a more delicious variety of insect choices for her dining pleasure. But then, I would reason, she is safe where she is. Safe inside her little screen, protected from predators, strong winds, and the torrential soaking rains that might wash an itsy bitsy spider out. She was safe, and in truth, if she wanted to and had tried at all, she easily could have found a gap in the screen and made her way out into the world. No, she seemed to be content enough, choosing the safe, if mundane, life.

And mundane it was. That little dudelette really didn't do much. Morning, noon, and night she was more or less in the same spot, hanging upside down waiting for a tremble in her web that signaled dinner had arrived.

I had gotten used to my little amiga over the course of the summer, so even though it was beginning to cool off, I had not opened that door because her web was woven between the screen drape and the door, and I didn't want to tear it apart.

During the past couple of months, I have spent a lot of time thinking and writing, writing and thinking. Moving this slowly toward the end of a long marriage leads (for me, at least) to spending as much time as possible being with all the thoughts and feelings that come with such an important step. I have now spent seven years married but separated. Not in, but not out. Alone but not independent. Disconnected but not free. Hanging on to a gossamer thread of relationship, afraid to let go because it felt safe. Well, not safe exactly, but safer. Safer than whatever else was out there. Safer than the unknown.

And then one day, a minor emotional storm blew through and shook the foundation of my self-doubt. Shook it right out from under me. In a moment of crystal clarity, I realized what a shocking disservice I was doing to myself. I realized I was living behind a screen drape. I could see the world beyond and pretend to be in it, but I was safe inside the buffer zone of "married," while playing in the fake freedom of "separated." By holding on to this skeleton of a marriage, I was effectively putting my entire life on hold. Not because I thought we might be able to reconcile—that was never an option—but because I was too scared to see what life was like when it was wholly and completely my own. Is this what I wanted? To live like that spider, hanging on the inside of the screen, waiting for life to happen to me? Seeing the roses but only from a distance? Feeling the sun, but only reflected off the ground? Sensing the breeze, but never feeling its full force? Knowing it's raining, but never really having to get wet? Waiting for some tiny dropperful of life that might just happen to find its way into my safe little screened-in world?

The next day I told my husband we had to move forward with divorce.

Within a couple of weeks of this decision, we had one of those Texas storms that leaves a degree of damage that has people asking, "Are they sure a tornado didn't touch down?" Trees torn up from the roots, others split in half, with the massive trunks contorted in ways only circular winds could create. Roofs torn off, and tens of thousands of people without power for days. In my little enclave we didn't get the worst of it, but the winds were very strong. The next day, I noticed a tendril of the variegated ivy that arches over my bedroom doorway had blown inside one of the gaps in the screen drape during the storm. My little spider was still hanging out, having been held safe from the storm by her screen, but the tip of the ivy tendril had landed within two inches of her preferred spot. It would have been the easiest thing in the world for her to step out onto that ivy and walk out of her self-imposed prison. It was right there, offered to her like a variegated stairway to freedom.

For a couple of days nothing changed. They hung together, spider and ivy. Neither moved. But then one day, when I woke up and sat down in my big brown chair with my morning tea, I looked over and my little spider was gone. The only thing left was the ivy invitation.

I believe she took it.

Chapter 4

Emergence

Víbora

There is upheaval going on in my garden and in my life. The west fence fell down in a storm and needs to be replaced, but in the process, my entire west garden has been wrecked. Once the fence was gone, I discovered both large mulberry trees, which drew hundreds of migrating birds for sustenance each year, were rotted at the base and had to come down. And worse, my ancient, epic trumpet vine where the travelers rested and the hummingbirds danced, the trumpet vine that arched over the west pathway, creating a beautiful flower tunnel inviting guests deeper into my garden, had also been destroyed.

I've had a love/hate relationship with that trumpet vine for years. On the one hand, it was beautiful and huge, with artfully twisting and draping vines that gave age and mystery to my garden. And that natural archway...oh, what an exquisite example of nature as architect! I truly adored it. On the other hand, the vine was so invasive. I was constantly fighting tiny, tenacious trumpet vines all over my garden, even in the front yard, which is almost half an acre away! And trumpet vines are tough. Their roots are sturdy and deep. Plus, it's orange. I don't love orange. I find it rather bossy, though as oranges go, this one was quieter than most. More importantly, it doesn't go with the palette of my garden, which is predominantly cooler shades of blues, greens, lavenders, purples, and silvers, with some deep, bright, and soft pinks. But as much as I have resented, despised, and cursed the trumpet vine at times, I have loved it with all my heart at others, and when I had to decide whether or not to cut it down when the fence fell, I fought with all my horticultural know-how and spent a small fortune trying to save it.

But in the end, it just wasn't possible. The replacement fence was being moved back four feet, so the vine would lose that support. Another portion of its weight had been held by the mulberry trees. Over the decades, vine and trees had woven together into a beautiful single unit. The mulberries guided the vine up through their branches, and it spilled out in every direction with hundreds of cascading orange blossoms—beacons for passing birds to the sumptuous bed and breakfast below in the whimsical garden. The mulberries were so intertwined with the trumpet vine, they looked like glorious, exotic flowering trees.

The day the mulberries were being removed, I had five

men working to reinforce the vine, which likely weighed fifteen hundred pounds, while four others cut the first tree. With an elaborate cat's cradle of ropes and pulleys, they managed to hold the vine at first. But when the second tree came down, releasing its portion of the vine, the added weight was more than the men could hold, and the vine collapsed. We just couldn't save it.

This most recent garden calamity triggered my resistance to letting things go. Sudden loss has been a theme in my life. In defense, I learned to hold on. I hold on because I'm afraid. Afraid of loss and the void it will create. So when the trumpet vine fell, all my conflicted feelings about it evaporated, and I cried because it felt like one more thing I didn't want to lose that was being taken away from me.

But now, it had to come out. The trumpet vine that hooked so artfully into the mulberry trees was right outside my bedroom doors. It was the view from which I drew inspiration as I sat in my big brown chair. It was the most beautiful view from my house, the place inside where I could feel outside. And now it was gone. So it took me a while to let it go. As the vine lay on the ground, and the days wore on, the same activity continued—birds perching, hummers humming, anoles snapping up bugs, bunnies hopping, fledglings fledging. Six cardinal babes and two tiny wrens learning about the world before me. I was so reluctant to cut it away, it took me a week to give the okay.

In the meantime, I had finally decided I was filing for divorce that week. Over seven years into our separation and at last I was done with the limbo. No more separation, I wanted to be divorced. So I had recently set events into motion to accomplish that, despite Dan's unexpected resistance to taking this final step. Almost magically, when I committed to divorcing, an internal shift happened, and I was ready to let go of loads of memories, furniture, china, photos, and personal items that I had clung to for decades. Beautiful things, but masses of them that filled my closets and cabinets and stuffed my garage to the ceiling. Boxes and boxes of things that belonged to other people. People I loved, but things *they* loved. Things that were suffocating me with the weight of their history and the felt responsibility of being the keeper for the dead. I had grappled with deep guilt about letting go of all the things that were loved by the people I loved. Until suddenly, I didn't.

It was in the midst of this seismic shift within me that the trumpet vine fell down. After I had cried for a while, and stared at it lying there on the ground for a few days, I got centered, pulled myself together, and said, "Okay, let's cut it back." My crew spent a couple of hours respectfully trimming the large tendrils by hand because I knew it was home to many critters and I didn't want them to go after it with a chain saw. The little ones needed time to fly or scamper away, and we needed to carefully scout for any nests or other baby casings so they could be moved. I had also decided I would try to preserve the main vine trunks and some of the major arching branches as a structure to support a new wisteria vine, so I oversaw the cutting back quite closely.

When they finished, I went back into my house and

looked at its bony remains from my chair. I watched a cardinal fledgling and the two little baby wrens explore the vine's new incarnation, hopping around on the naked branches that now bounced under the weight of their tiny bodies. It was surprisingly beautiful still. Big, contorting, twisting vines, wrist thick, tangling forth, still forming a truncated, sculptural, now somewhat more abstract arch. As I adjusted to this drastically modified view from my room, suddenly I saw an unfamiliar motion. A slow, even, undulating movement, almost like water flowing...upward. I jumped up and ran to the glass door, knowing at a visceral level what it was before my mind could catch up to my amygdala. It was a snake. A really, *really* big snake.

I grabbed my phone and my good camera and ran outside. This puppy was huge by non-jungle standards, easily seven or eight feet long and as big around as a roll of Christmas wrapping paper. I have lived here for a lot of years, and I have never seen anything other than tiny garter snakes in my garden before, but this was definitely not that!

I snapped some quick pictures with my phone and threw them up on Facebook. I needed an ID and I needed it fast. I knew there were only a few kinds of venomous snakes in Texas, and I knew how to identify them by their head shape, and I knew for sure this wasn't a rattlesnake, but I didn't know what it was. I also knew my crew would want to kill it no matter what. We have had some harsh words over the killing of tiny garden snakes in the past. But they have had some bad experiences with snakes, so I needed proof it wasn't dangerous. I ran inside to look it up myself, but before I could even get online, my sister in California had an ID, which she posted on my Facebook wall: "Texas rat snake. Aggressive but not poisonous."

Now I would just like to take a moment to say, yeah, yeah, yeah, I'm Nature Girl and all that. But very large snakes do make me nervous. Not panicked, not frightened, but definitely nervous. A colleague quickly supported my sister's ID online: "Rat snake, scary looking but not dangerous."

I went back outside and took dozens more pictures. Camo Snake, as I was calling her at the time, moved slowly along the tangles of the bare trumpet vine, then stopped to consider me for many minutes as I snapped away and gazed at her in curious, nervous wonder. She would move again, I would watch and snap, then she would stop and consider me again. On several occasions, our eyes met and we held each other's gaze for longer than I felt fully comfortable. But each time, her caution seemed to ease as I consciously managed my energy to be calm and nonthreatening. Eventually, she moved to a high, open, sunlit branch. From this position, I could see an odd contour to her body. A rippling wave of swells and cinches that made me wonder if she might be pregnant. Or maybe she had just had dinner, who knows. But I decided to lower my camera and I spoke to her. She never took her eyes off me as I spoke. I told her there was nothing to fear from me and I wouldn't let my crew hurt her either. I told her I needed her to agree not to bother them or me and I would protect her. I asked her to please not eat my baby garden bunnies or my baby birds, but she could have all the rats she wanted. Everybody's gotta eat.

When I finished, I thanked her and wished her well. I then went down the side of my house to the Blue Garden to tell the crew not to bother her. *Víbora*, they called her. Spanish for snake.

"What a pretty word," I said.

"I don't like it," Fernando replied. "It means problems."

"Not this time." I smiled.

They were skeptical, but agreed.

I was only with them two or three minutes, but when I returned to the vine remains, Víbora was gone. I was upholding my end of the bargain, so I guess she was upholding hers. I've never seen her again.

Many cultures now and historically hold a far different view of snakes than ours in the West. In mythology, the snake symbolizes fertility, wisdom, death, and resurrection. Children born in the Year of the Snake in Asia are said to be humorous, sophisticated, calm, and independent. The ancient Egyptians worshipped the cobra, and even today Hindus consider snakes divine, as they represent eternity and impermanence. This parallels some Western native traditions that believe snakes symbolize the end of one phase of your life and herald a wiser awakening—death and resurrection, transformation and healing. Snake guides point us toward wholeness, consciousness, and an ability to release resistance and be open to a new way of being, as snake heralds the coming of change. Snake wisdom assures us we need not fear this change—we are safe, for as a spirit guide, it appears when we seek support as we step out into the unknown. Not much resonance there.

Perhaps my encounter with Víbora was just a chance brush with a very large, very unusual wild creature in my garden. But in all the time I've owned this house and this garden, the one and only moment that I have ever laid eyes on, let alone come within a foot of a gigantic, universal symbol of death, release, resurrection, transformation, and rebirth was on the exact week I filed for divorce after all these years...? I think that's more of a confirmation than a coincidence.

The Rescue

A storm was building. It seemed out of the blue, but then, I don't keep track of the weather like you might expect a landscape designer to do. So as usual, I had no idea this storm was coming until the first crack of thunder. I ran to the window, and sure enough, extremely dark, billowing clouds were blowing in fast. Something was definitely about to go down, so I hurried outside to catch the show.

I love a good storm, and it's a good thing because we get a lot of them. When storms come in around here, they can really be something. I positioned myself in the middle of my garden so I could see all around the sky. This storm seemed to be coming in from every direction. It looked like it was going to be a doozy! I find it mesmerizing to watch storm clouds. Not so much regular clouds, but storm clouds are so pregnant, filled with uncertainty, electricity, and even possible danger. They are dark and unpredictable and sometimes rough, but after they pass, the garden is so fresh and green and clean, not just washed by the rain, but fed and truly cleansed by it.

Of course, the metaphor is not lost on me either. I have certainly learned by now that I can't predict or stop the storms that blow into my life, but no matter their degree of difficulty, in the end, each one has brought new wisdom that is both deepening and expanding. I was actually thinking about that very thing as I watched this particular storm blow in, since I had just committed to filing for divorce days before, after years of my life hanging in suspended animation while I allowed fear, self-doubt, and inertia to hold me in a state of perpetual limbo for far too long.

A bright flash of lightning right over my head, followed almost instantly by a deafening crack of thunder, made me jump. The storm was no longer coming in; it was here. I am always a little disappointed when the first raindrops fall, because I'm never ready to go inside when there's a storm outside. So often, I sit in the rain for as long as I can before I have to retreat, but this time it was late and I was hungry.

I went into the kitchen and made a salad as the rain really kicked in. Within minutes it went from a sprinkle to hard rain, and became a deluge in a hurry. This one was indeed a doozy, so I thought it would be fun to go outside and eat dinner on my covered porch, which is the next best thing to actually being in the storm. It was kind of crowded out there because I had a lot of plants in containers lined up waiting for an installation, but I could still get to my comfy chair, which I had already pulled back from the edge of the porch so it wouldn't get wet. We had been in a drought for a while, so I was excited to have a chance to surround myself in the storm. The rain was coming down in torrents and was quickly accumulating in the low areas of the garden. This was a gully washer for sure. It was darker than a normal dusk because of the storm so it was a bit hard to see, but as I approached the double glass doors of my living room to go out onto the porch, something skittered across the porch floor right in front of me. It was quick and I only caught the tail end of it (so to speak), but I was pretty sure that was the tail end of a rat.

Annoyance hit. "Are you kidding?!" I thought. After my close encounter with the giant rat snake only a couple of days before, I'm a little ashamed to admit my next thought was, "Where's the rat snake when you need it?" but almost simultaneously with that thought I noticed something unusual about the behavior of this particular rat. When I first came to the door, it was disappearing into the woodpile right up next to the house, but before I could react, it bolted back out into the rain. Only a minute later, it was hurrying back to the woodpile at more of a trot, then dashed back out into the rain. There was definite urgency to its gait.

This was a rat on a mission. The second time it appeared, I thought I could see something in its mouth, but as I said, it was getting dark, and I wasn't sure. The third time the rat returned, gingerly running to the woodpile, then running hard back out into the rain, I was sure I was watching a rescue mission. I stood very still because by now compassion had swept over me. This was a mother desperately trying to save her babies.

She turned again and ran back out into the storm. The rain was coming down hard and fast, and the water was rising past the edge of my porch and beginning to flood the first few feet inside. This was a flash flood, and I knew that if it lasted long, even the woodpile wouldn't be safe.

Mama rat was undeterred. She dodged full speed through the plants on the porch and forged through the deep water like a triathlete because time was not on her side. I don't know where her nest was, but her babies were clearly in imminent peril and were helpless without her. Four babies later, she stopped. Either all babies were present and accounted for, or her nest was underwater and it was too late for the rest. She paused, then retreated to shelter in the plant pots nearby, and I finally moved. I ran to get my camera and opened the door to the porch slowly so as not to alarm her. I could see her tucked in the plants just a few feet away, catching her breath and licking herself to dry off. I walked cautiously out and over to the woodpile, watching her from the corner of my eye. She was watching me, too. As I neared the woodpile, she froze.

"It's okay," I said quietly. "I just want to look."

Sure enough, there they were. Four tiny newborn ratlettes, completely hairless, eyes closed, probably only hours old. I snapped a few pictures and left them in peace. As if giving birth isn't hard enough without then having to immediately save the lives of your entire brood from a flash flood. I had a strong urge to comfort her, or feed her or something, but then I decided what she really needed was just to be left alone.

When I came inside, I couldn't stop thinking about mama rat and her babies. About the perils of day-to-day life, about how everything around you can change in an instant, about the passion and sacrifices of motherhood, about how one minute I was wishing for a rat snake and the next I was doing what I could to offer her calm energy and a safe haven for her family. And about how this related to my own life. How interesting that only two days prior, I was presented with a gigantic snake in my garden and today, a small mother, another symbol of birth and renewal brought to me by creatures that, in a vacuum, cause fear and revulsion, and many want to destroy.

In some cultures, rats symbolize wealth and abundance. In others they represent resourcefulness, as they are clever survivors. Earth-based cultures say rats (like snakes) mark a time of change and new beginnings. Rat messengers offer support during times of emotional upheaval and an opportunity to declutter everything that no longer serves you, including relationships, feelings, and outdated beliefs. Rat spirit guides can help you examine the emotional burdens you carry, and help you transform fear into courage.

And mother rat? Mother rat, with babies in peril? Well,

I'm no shaman, but my intuition says that as I take this step forward into the process of divorcing, scary though it is, I am protected, safe, nurtured, cared for, and loved. I don't know if that's what it means. But that's what I need, so I'm going with it.

Patita

The world is a mysterious place. A lot of people devote a great deal of time and energy trying to understand the world and our place in it. I am one of those people. But lately, I have begun to settle into a still uneasy peace around the reality that much of our world is unknowable. At least for me. At least for now.

But there are a few things I think I have figured out. One of them is that a tremendous amount of our suffering in life comes from our belief in a fair and just world. Our belief in a contract between us and the Universe. A fundamental agreement that suggests if we are good people and do the right thing, goodness will be returned to us. Goodness, and most important, that elusive jewel we call happiness. Of course, we come by this belief honestly. The pervasive themes contained in the texts of most religions throughout the ages tell us that if we do the right thing, we will go to Heaven or Jannah or Elysium or Valhalla or Xanadu or Nirvana or the Third Realm or somewhere that is beautiful, peaceful, and free of suffering. But this contract also implies that goodness is returned to us here and now, and the truth is, that just simply is not always the case.

Mind you, I am not the first person to figure this out. Subtle clues are out there everywhere cautioning us not to get attached to the idea that being good has a high rate of return on investment—phrases like "kindness is its own reward" (read: don't expect anything back from this), "when bad things happen to good people" (because that clearly needs explaining), not to mention the book of Job. All of which seems like a huge disappointment, until you can cobble together a shift in perspective. And my personal perspective shift is unfurling in the form of a gentle release from the need to understand everything. An embrace of the mystery. My curiosity remains, and my exploration will continue, but I have realized that my thesis needs to change. Instead of looking for proof of a fair and just world, I need to accept that the world is a neutral place. That makes understanding a lot easier, because proof of *that* is everywhere.

One of the mysteries that piques my interest and curiosity is the similarities and differences in world religions, and the spiritual practices of tribal, indigenous, and ancient cultures. I don't believe in astrology or shamanism per se, but I don't *not* believe in them either. I can't explain them, and they feel quite fringe to me much of the time, but they have been trusted for millennia, and it is fascinating how right they often are. One thing I fully believe is that there is much about our world, the cosmos, and our connection to them that we do not understand. I also believe that there is more of a crossover between science and spirituality than might be readily apparent. I am a very curious person who does not easily accept vague explanations that do not actually give answers to some of the greater questions I have about life, so I choose to be open to things, particularly in the natural world, that are oddly accurate despite my having no way to explain them.

Like this week, for example. Having now committed to divorcing Daniel, hired a lawyer, filed the paperwork, and begun to attend to the details of that process, I was feeling pretty grounded in the state of that relationship. My situation with Glenn, however, was another matter.

At this point in our lives, Glenn and I had different priorities. I was in survival mode, and as much as I loved him, committing my whole future to anyone seemed far too big to get my head around. But Glenn was in love for the first time, and he wanted that nailed down. He wanted a commitment. I said I wasn't ready. I said I didn't know what I wanted. I said he was too young for me. I said he was too far away. I said I needed to figure out who I was. I said my priority was to figure out how to support myself financially. I said a lot of things, and all of them were at least partially true. But the real truth...the big truth...the driving truth was I was scared and had no clue how to be with someone who loved me as much as he did. Glenn, on the other hand, knew exactly what he wanted. He wanted me. Until death do us part.

Because of this ongoing struggle over the nature of our relationship, we went through some extremely difficult times. He got jealous, and I lashed out at him for trying to control me. He felt hurt, and I accused him of trying to manipulate me. The more he tried to move toward me and establish a deeper, more permanent relationship, the more I set what I called boundaries. I thought I was choosing myself. I said I was standing in my power. I insisted I was claiming my independence. But this isn't what standing in power and independence looks like. I know that now. This was me reacting against things my husband had done during our marriage and overlaying them onto Glenn. These were not actions, but reactions. Backlash from decades of powerlessness. Then I did what the powerless often do when the tables turn. I exercised power the same way it had been used against me, by abusing it. In trying to stand up for myself, I unintentionally routed a beautiful love affair with a rare, precious young man because I couldn't handle the depth, intensity, and guilelessness of his love. I was trying to protect myself, but I had done it badly, awkwardly, unconsciously, unfairly, and sometimes even unkindly. And the truth is, I thought he would always be there. He said he would, and I believed him.

During this time, because he was hurt, Glenn had succumbed to a shamelessly persistent girl whose anaconda grip was making things much more complicated. Disagreements and quarrels turned into outright conflict as Anaconda tried to drive a wedge between us and stake a claim, furthering our problems. Torn between his complicated, inconvenient, and often frustrating love for me, and the convenience, simplicity, and omnipresent persistence of Anaconda the Barnacle Girl, Glenn had begun living a dual existence. I discovered him lying to me about her on numerous occasions, and I was in turmoil about what to do about it.

Over the years, he had been such a touchstone for me. He helped me heal so much of the emotional damage from my childhood and my marriage. He helped restore my connection with my heart, my body, and my sexuality, as well as my belief in the possibility of a deep, loving soul connection. The permission I had to be completely authentic with Glenn was profound. No matter how I showed up, he loved me. Through Glenn's love, I realized what a narrow corridor of permission to be myself I was allowed with Dan, who didn't want me to be too bright, too outgoing, too glamourous, too successful, or too sexual. However, neither could I be too reserved, too quiet, too sad, too angry, too passive, too unhappy, or not sexual enough. And I certainly couldn't be too heavy. Glenn allowed me to expand into my fullness. He loved my mind, my wisdom, my heart, my sensitivity, and my body, while also holding space with compassion for my messiness, smallness, pettiness, fear, and anger. The world of self-expression had grown so big with Glenn, I was rattling around in it, trying to figure out how to be in this new, spacious realm.

He understood when my wounds were activated, and he never judged me for it. He always saw me as my highest expression because he always looked at me through the eyes of love. The safety his love provided me was immeasurable. With Glenn, I was able to access my brightest light and my darkest inclinations. With Glenn, I could be real, without pretense or the need to please or impress. "I absolutely love you, and I love you absolutely" was his mantra with me. And he showed me for years the depth of that truth.

But now, our relationship is shifting. My resistance to commitment with him is coming back to haunt me, and I am swimming in grief and regret. He and I had an agreement that since we lived so far apart, if we ever went out with anyone else, we would keep it light. But apparently, although he repeatedly told Anaconda he was not attracted to her "in that way" and was in no way interested in a relationship with her, he failed to tell her why. So even though she knew he wasn't that into her, it turned out she had been willing to be his "friend with benefits" for almost two years. And while he was playing checkers, she was playing chess. In time, she declared her past benefits should have a cumulative credit of significantly more than the face value of the ticket, and she had begun to apply steady, focused pressure on him to say he loved her and make their relationship official and exclusive. Already in way too deep, he had been incrementally succumbing to her demands while continually lying by omission to her about me, and lying outright to me about her.

So, this is the part where everybody who isn't me says, "Seriously...? You didn't see that coming?"

No. I didn't see it coming. I didn't see it coming because I trusted him. I knew he was seeing her, but I had told him I didn't want any details about her or anyone else he dated because I knew it would upset me. Besides, when he did talk about her, it wasn't very flattering. He said not to worry, so I didn't. I loved him very much, but the details of my life and the details of us were too complicated for me to sort out concurrently with the end of my marriage, the beginning of building my business, diving into my history of abuse, and healing a thousand wounds to my spirit. I only have so much bandwidth. And did I mention—*I trusted him*. I trusted him to keep the agreement we had made until we changed that agreement. At some level, I always knew some kind of conclusion to our relationship was probably inevitable, but I didn't expect it to be like this, and when it began to happen, I felt like I had been flayed and cast into a vat of acid. All my abandonment and betrayal wounds were being ignited to the max. I was lashing out with fury that was so strong he was crumbling under the weight of my emotions. We would make decisions to redefine our relationship, then see each other and be overtaken by our deep love and passion, and determine to figure out a way. The truth was, we had to reframe our relationship. But trying to put that into practice was tearing us both to shreds. And it was very, very messy.

One day, when I was in a particularly anguished place about this, I was sitting in the beautiful shaded backyard of a job site as my crew was putting the finishing touches on the design installation. The garden overhung a creek whose banks were solidly covered in wild violets. As I sat in this lovely setting, my heart breaking and completely absorbed in my despair, I looked up, and directly ahead of me a duck was walking through the side gate into the garden, headed straight for me. I sat very still, watching her as she waddled up to me. I greeted her softly when she arrived, and she gave me a gurgling quack in reply. Then she positioned herself right next to me. I was puzzled. She poodled around me rooting in the flower beds and pecking at the ground, but never wandered more than three or four feet away from me. For a while, I tried to be still, but then I realized she didn't care if I was still or not. She was just doing her little duck thing, and hanging out with me. I got up and went over to talk to Fernando for a moment, and she waddled over there with me. I came back to the step where I had been sitting, and she waddled back with me. I decided to move to a more comfortable place, and she tagged along. I chatted her up a little, and she made soft quacking sounds back. Every so often she would walk up to me, look me in the eyes, and hold my gaze for a long while. At one point I thought she might sit on my foot. It seemed as if at any time, I could have reached down, picked her up, put her in my lap, and she would have just snuggled in. Any bystander would have thought for sure that she was my pet duck. It was the most bizarre wildlife encounter I had ever experienced.

This went on all day. The crew would come over and

work around us, or ask me questions, and my little duck was unfazed. *"Patita,"* they called her. A diminutive in Spanish for female duck. I went to pick up lunch for the crew, and she followed me to the gate, then waited there until I got back, and followed me back into the garden. Throughout the day, wherever I wanted to sit, she padded after me and took up residence beside me. She was a pretty little mallard, mostly brown with a glorious shock of iridescent bluish purple on her sides. When the light caught her just right, the color shimmered. It was somehow more startlingly beautiful for being surrounded by the subtle browns of the rest of her feathers. That evening, when it was time to go home, I felt really quite sad, almost as if I were abandoning her.

Because ducks are associated with water, they reflect feminine energy. This ties them to the emotional states, and invites us to be sure we are taking care of ourselves, protecting our hearts, and not always putting our own needs aside in deference to the needs of others. Brown-feathered ducks like Patita help ground us in periods of change, growth, and ultimately healing, while the iridescent purple feathers on her sides suggest a search for emotional security. Ducks are graceful and demonstrate by example how to navigate through painful challenges with grace.

Vicki, the homeowner, told me Patita stayed the night, then around midday the next day, she flew away.

The world is a mysterious place. I may never truly understand why Patita came to stay with me for a day when I needed her. I will certainly never understand how she might have known I needed her. John Muir wrote, "When we try to pick out anything [in nature] by itself, we find that it is bound fast by a thousand invisible cords that cannot be broken, to everything else in the universe." I choose to believe that Patita and I are proof of that.

Seasons of Love

Eight years. That's not an insignificant amount of time to be in a relationship with someone. And it is a really long time to be half-in and half-out of a relationship. Let alone two of them. But that was me. I was always half-in and half-out with Glenn, and I had been half-in and half-out with Daniel, too, all the years we were separated. The years weren't wasted, though. I've grown a lot. More in some areas than others to be sure, but on balance, I think it's safe to say that I am in no way the same person I was the day Daniel moved out.

People can surprise you. Indeed, I think that if you stick around long enough, people will almost always surprise you, one way or another. Dan surprised me when he asked for a divorce and moved out. Then he surprised me when he told me about Jane, and he surprised me again the night he told me that he couldn't imagine how high I could fly without his wet blanket. I thought I knew Dan, but I didn't. Not really.

I thought I knew Glenn, too, but he surprised me as well. Twice.

It's times like these when that issue I have about not being able to let go becomes a real problem. The situation with Glenn had continued to deteriorate as pressures in his life outside of his relationships took a toll on his resiliency. He continued to fail to meet his agreements with me while also feeling ill equipped to fend off Anaconda's tantrums and demands. So I made the decision to transition our relationship into one of just friends. He could have that drama-addicted woman-child. And good luck with that. We had agreed in advance that we both wanted to formalize this transition in a loving way, so we planned a ceremony of release to honor the beauty and wonder of what we had been to each other, and then to welcome a new way of being together. He flew down to me. We agreed to spend the first few days in closure, enjoying one another as lovers; then we would sit in ceremony together, sharing what we loved about each other, the gratitude we felt for each other, and speaking into the room what we were willing to release. Then we planned to spend the next few days experiencing this new way of being together before he went home. It was all going to be very loving, very civilized, and very adult. In my heart I had already made peace with this change of status.

The first few days together were filled with hours of love-making, deep conversations, laughter, and magic, as always. On the third day, we agreed not to have any alcohol and to eat lightly so we could be fully present for the ceremony that night. We arranged an altar in my living room because everything about our love felt sacred. He brought mementos with him from our years together to place on the altar—one of many romantic, thoughtful things he often did that made me love him so much. We lit candles, sat down together, and turned to face each other. He took my hands and looked into my eyes for a long time. Then he spoke first.

"I don't want this. I know I agreed, but I don't want to do this. I love you. You are my soul mate. You are my dream. You are my one and only true love. I don't know what I am doing with her. I don't love her. Half the time I don't even like her that much. I love *you*. You are my everything. I can't imagine my life without you, and I do not want to do this. I know what I want to do. I want to devote myself to you. I promise, I will stop seeing her. It won't even be hard. Please...please let's not do this."

"I'll still be here," I said. "We'll still be friends. Close friends. Best friends. That part won't change."

"No, that's not what I want. I want to spend my life with you. I want to dedicate myself to you and to us. You're all I've ever wanted. I don't want to live without you. I don't want to be just friends. Please..."

As he spoke, I felt my heart sink. I truly had not expected this. I had made peace with transitioning our relationship. I was ready to do that. I wanted to do it. But it's hard to say no when someone you still love is begging you to stay. At least, it was hard for me. So, against my better judgment, I agreed, on the condition he make good on his promises.

He finally managed to end things with Anaconda after weeks of her histrionics, anger, pleading, and a complete abandonment of any self-respect she may have had. But over the next few months, there was rising evidence that she had been slithering back into the picture. To save face, she had gotten him to agree to lie to their friends, saying they mutually decided to split up, so she could continue to be around him. Group photos showed her still stuck to him like a leaf gall. I asked for his reassurances a few times, which he readily gave, but I was too consumed with ensuring my company could be a viable financial resource and trying to manage my fragmented life to give what was going on in Canada much attention. I was working seventy-hour weeks, simultaneously installing multiple big projects, and any spare time was monopolized by the difficult, emotionally taxing details of finalizing my divorce. I didn't have a millimeter of bandwidth left to monitor whether or not Glenn was living up to promises that he had freely and passionately offered to me.

If my marriage to Dan were a season, it would be summer. Summer in Texas. Big, beautiful blue skies and white puffy clouds early on, but as time passed it kept getting hotter. The heat never let up, there was no relief in sight, and in such conditions, little could survive.

Our divorce was final the morning of December 17. After so many years of being in suspended animation, the push to draw it to a close before Christmas made the end feel sudden. By that morning, much of the healing work I had been doing paid off. There was no animosity remaining in me toward Daniel. I felt nostalgic. Sad, even, after years and years of resentment. And grateful, not only for the lessons learned, but for the time he had given me to learn them. Also grateful and deeply relieved because we had decided I would get to keep the house and my beloved garden, which could not have happened without his generosity in our settlement agreement.

The court proceeding was a strangely quick formality. An assembly line of changed and broken hearts. When my lawyer and I left the courtroom, she turned to me and said, "I have been practicing family law for over twenty-five years, and I have never seen two people be kinder to each other." I'm proud of that. And grateful for it, as well.

Although Dan and Jane didn't last, he seems to have found a lovely woman now who sounds perfect for him. My son tells me I would probably like her a lot. I genuinely hope they are happy.

If my time with Glenn were a season, it would be spring. Spring in Texas. It was a time of rebirth where everything felt new and beautiful and full of promise. In the arms of Glenn's love I was able to grow, and I could bud and bloom on that new growth. It was beautiful while it lasted, but spring is short-lived in Texas. And it includes tornado season.

Less than two weeks after my divorce was final, Glenn and I met in Montreal for my birthday and New Year's Eve. Something was off, but I was too emotionally and physically exhausted by the relentless stress of the year to focus on it. He had sent a huge arrangement of several dozen red roses, which was waiting for me in the hotel room when I arrived—the same hotel and the same room in which we had stayed the weekend we first met in person, all those years before. On New Year's Eve, we watched fireworks over the Saint Lawrence River from our window, then went outside and strolled under sparkling Christmas lights strung overhead to the celebratory sounds of a band on the dock, weaving through street vendors and festive crowds. It was the first time we had ever been together when I was completely and totally free. I expected it to feel different, and it did, though not in the way I had anticipated.

We had stopped by Dallas for a couple of days after we left Montreal to pick up my car; then we were going to drive to Santa Fe together. Glenn loved being in my home. He often told me it was the safest place he had ever felt. Winter at my house meant time in the hot tub, and hours together on a faux fur blanket in front of a roaring fire in the fireplace, with my cats curled up nearby. Pretty much our idea of Heaven. Glenn was really looking forward to this part of our trip. I like to spend as much time as possible in New Mexico. I had told him so much about the beauty and unique style of this state I loved, and was anxious to share it with him. The morning before we were to leave for New Mexico, Glenn was in the living room, and I was making up the bed. At the very moment I went around to his side, a message flashed up on his phone. It was from her. It was obviously a continuation of an ongoing conversation, and it was clearly not from someone who was just a friend. I took a few stunned steps into the middle of my room. He walked in. He asked what was wrong. I gestured back toward his phone. He asked if she had messaged him. I said yes. He walked over and got his phone and said, "Well, she has been messaging me, but I haven't responded."

I said, "I don't believe you."

He said, "I'm sorry you don't believe me, but it's true."

I said, "Really? Show me your phone."

He said, "I don't see the point in that."

I said, "Let me get this straight. You hold in your hand the means by which you can prove to me that you are not lying, *and you don't see the point in that?*"

After a short but intense argument, at my insistence, he handed me his phone. Stupidest idea I've ever had. I scrolled through their conversations in complete disbelief. He was, in fact, reaping her benefits again, and to appease her deep insecurity about me, he had slandered me with every fear I ever confided in him.

It's worth noting for historical reference that I am not a screamer. I don't scream, I don't yell, I don't call people names, I don't say vicious things I will later regret. Basically, I don't really fight. I can argue, but my very limited access to anger up to this point only presented in the form of cutting sarcasm, flawless logic, and piercing, diminishing analogies. Any venting always happened in hindsight with friends—never to the target audience—and even then, it never included raised voices. Not once did Daniel or I ever yell at each other over the years when our marriage was dissolving, nor while we were separated. This pearl is worth knowing because when I read her vulgar messages and saw the tasteless selfies she was sending him,

I.

Went.

Postal.

I don't remember the details of when I went postal. I just know that I went completely off the rails. For three days. That's right, for three days, I was screaming, and roaring, and swearing, and crying, and lashing out with every furious, cruel, cutting thought that popped into my head. I was completely without filters. Nothing was too mean. No insult too low. I said things I meant and things I didn't mean, but if I thought it would hurt him, I didn't care if it was true. I verbally eviscerated both him and her in as many ways as I could think of, and *believe me*, I could think of many, many ways. Honestly, I now understand crimes of passion. I do. I don't condone them, but I completely understand now how someone can be so angry they lose control and do something unspeakably terrible, even deadly. During those three days, every repressed and suppressed ounce of rage that I had held inside for over five decades came flying out of me with the force of Drogon, Rhaegal, and Viserion combined. I had never yelled at anyone in my whole life before. Not Daniel, not Julia, not Bon Bon, not anyone. It all came out at Glenn.

And he took it. He stayed, he cried, he apologized, he begged for forgiveness, and he took it. He emailed her and told her everything—his lack of feelings for her, his love for me, all his lies, and his many promises made and broken. He tried to fix it. He tried to fix us. But there were no pieces to reassemble. This relationship had vaporized.

When the car arrived to take Glenn to the airport, my parting words were "I'll never see you again." His parting words to me were "I don't believe that. I won't believe that. I can't believe that."

I was so grateful that my marriage to Dan was able to end peacefully and develop into a friendship. I tried to save what was most valuable with Glenn, but I wasn't strong enough to stick to my decision at our transition ceremony, and now, one of the most treasured loves of my life is lost.

They say that people come into our lives for a reason, a season, or a lifetime. If there are five hundred twenty-five thousand six hundred minutes in a year, then Glenn and I had over 4 million minutes together. But if we measure in love, and love is eternal, then we have eternity together. Maybe I will be able to forgive him by then.

Coyote Ugly

My plans to spend ten days in Santa Fe with Glenn changed hard and fast. I told him he had to leave, so he flew back to Toronto from Dallas, and I got in the car and drove past Santa Fe, straight to Taos. The timing of this couldn't have been worse, although I expect there is never a time when we would willingly put heartbreak, treachery, and total ego death on our calendar. But this particular block of time had been set aside for me to go into solitude, to process the final completion of my marriage, separation, and divorce, to consider what future might now be possible with Glenn, and to begin making plans for my new life. Instead, I found myself unable to do anything but rehash the last few days, while being emotionally flung about like a rabbit in the jaws of a wolf between fury, devastation, incredulity, sadness, and back into fury. It wasn't that I couldn't have seen this coming. I could have. I should have. I even kind of did. I just didn't want to fully face it. The signs were all there, but I so desperately wanted it to be different. "There are none so blind as those who will not see" the saying goes. Yep. That was me.

Sitting in my solitary retreat on the remote New Mexican mesa, the land softly undulating up to the Sangre de Cristo mountains, surrounded by little other than the wave of topography, dormant sagebrush, and the glistening white reverse shadows created by snow unmelted on the north side of each shrub, I am struck by the desolate beauty of this place. There is so little here, and yet it falls into harmony with the land so seamlessly its beauty is undeniable. It is deep winter, but it has been unseasonably mild, so rather than being covered by many established feet of snow, the ground lies dormant but bare. The colors are muted as if bathed in a pale sepia wash. Soft grays, tans, silvers, and beiges support ivory seed heads on dry, sleeping shrubs. No one cuts back their perennials in the winter here, so the skeletal remains of summer's flourish are bent over now, desiccate but still lovely, leaving form and texture as the garden's only expression.

I am always so pleased when wild critters come to call, and I admit I have been a little disappointed by the lack of fauna on this retreat. One bunny was all that had come a-nibbling at the dry, weedy offerings in this New Mexican winter's garden. But each day he came and seemed unafraid, so I was happy for that, at least. Far off in the distance one night, I thought I heard coyotes singing and wondered if I would see any, but it was a passing thought, as it was quickly followed by concern for my one daily visitor who would be nothing less than a tender morsel for a coyote.

Then one morning, early, as I was drinking my tea, a large, very healthy coyote sauntered right past my window. He was not in much of a hurry, pausing dead center outside my floor-to-ceiling wall of windows, giving me a fantastic view. If I had been outside, he would have been no more than ten to twelve feet away from me. He turned and looked straight at me for a moment, but then his attention was caught by a sound or movement through the sagebrush to the east, and he turned and trotted quickly toward it. I was thrilled but also annoyed that I didn't have my phone anywhere near so I could snap a picture of him. This compulsion being the evolution of humanity since the advent of social media.

I went about my business, and after a short time, he returned. This time I was ready! I jumped up and ran to the wall of windows to get a better view, snapped a few pictures as he moved slowly west, then ran into the bedroom to follow his path. From there I was so close to him, I could see the color gradation of his coat and was captivated by how perfectly he blended in with the environment. He was big and gorgeous, obviously very well fed. As his path curved around the house, I followed, watching from the windows on the west wall. He hopped over sage and other native plants, and from the corner of my eye I realized he was not alone. He was being joined by two other coyotes who were coming around the back of my house. Coyotes are known for their cleverness, and this pack, like velociraptors, was creating a circular trap as they hunted their prey.

I snapped away, and as I did, one of them noticed me. I lowered my camera as he stopped and held my gaze for a long moment. For a few steps, he approached me, alert and curious, never losing eye contact. I met his gaze and held it, too, fascinated by his brazen poise, then, unfazed, he turned and gamboled on across the range, rejoining the pack in their search for food.

I sat down and thought about my coyote encounter. How boldly they owned the land. How the pack had surrounded my house without my awareness. How seamlessly they melted into their environment, and how easy it would have been to miss them altogether, save for my attention, and their blatant fearlessness.

The power of coyote symbolism feels amplified here, as I am immersed in the heart of sacred Native American land. Coyotes invite us to look at something we have been avoiding, and if we resist looking at the truth, they will continue to intensify that invitation until we can no longer look the other way. Coyotes are associated with tricksters, and in addition to their own cleverness in avoiding traps, they also point out personal traps in which we might be caught. They are teachers who guide us to our sacred path, so if we are fooling ourselves about something or someone, coyote wants us to face the truth. And since it is in relationships where we can be the most selectively aware, and the most foolish... well, you get the picture.

Coyotes are bearers of the truth that needs to be seen. Sometimes the truth is ugly. My heart is broken, my trust is shattered, my belief in love is lost, but at least I'm finally willing to look.

March of the Sunflowers

Have you ever planted something you loved and wanted in your garden that subsequently took hold and began to self-propagate to the point where it became a nuisance? Where it choked and suffocated other plants you loved equally or even more, but somehow you couldn't quite bring yourself to stop it? I have. So many times. I've done it with reseeding larkspur, I've done it with reseeding datura, I've done it with rosemary that began as a four-inch pot and is now over fifteen feet in diameter, and I've done it with Knockout roses run amok. Probably other things, too. Those are just the ones I can think of at the moment whose determination outweighed my own. I even let some of my Knockout roses and that monster rosemary take over to the point that they shaded scores of irises into oblivion—irises that were some of my absolute favorite things in my garden. Why did I do that?

Have you ever lost yourself in a relationship? I've done that, too. So many times, in fact, that an objective observer might call it a pattern, or a habit...or a pathology. Truth be told, I can't remember a single intimate relationship where I haven't done this, and when I am really honest with myself, I can even see where I have done it with purely platonic friendships that meant a lot to me. I've allowed myself to be so completely immersed and overwhelmed by my passion and intensity in relationship that my own identity becomes a hazy blur. An abdication of individuality in favor of merging into the other that is so absolute, I am barely recognizable to myself. Not just unrecognizable, unfindable. I'm not sure why I keep doing it because it never turns out well. Never. I know it's not a good idea to make absolute statements, but this *never* turns out well.

I've got dozens of examples, the most recent of which is happening right now. I should've stuck with my plan and quit while I was ahead. But honestly...who does that? Who leaves when they're happy? And why would you? But hindsight being 20/20 and all, I definitely should have. Or at least cut bait when the handwriting started appearing on the wall...again. But no. Instead I hung in there like a frenzied wall washer, scrubbing out that handwriting as fast as it was appearing, and working with such focused dedication, I was barely aware of what I was doing myself. I mean, I knew what I was doing, I just couldn't or wouldn't see what effect it was going to have down the road. If I had been willing to look at the most likely outcome, I might have been able to see that a happy ending was impossible, or at least highly improbable. But I didn't want to know that. I was selectively oblivious to the reality of the direction the Glenn train was taking. So now, rather than ending with some semblance of dignity and shared love, we are hobbling away, shredded, broken, and permanently scarred. What a waste.

I can kind of forgive myself for being intoxicated by such an intoxicating young man. It was thrilling to be swept away by such wildly romantic notions as a love that had spanned lifetimes and could conquer all. I had a sense the future could hold challenges, but honestly, I've never been much of a planner. You know, the people with a one-year plan, a five-year plan, a ten-year plan, and a retirement plan? Yeah, that's not me. But, in the absence of thoughtful planning and conscious attention, nature takes its own course. Kind of like the march of the sunflowers in my garden.

One day, years ago, I pulled over on the side of a highway, clippers in hand, and cut an armload of wild sunflowers from a vacant lot I often drove past. When I got home, I put them in water, and when they expired a few days later, I took them out into my back garden and left the flower heads in a relatively open area of a flower bed, hoping seeds might form and take root in my garden. Sure enough, the next year, I had three gorgeous sunflower volunteers, right where I had left the spent blooms.

The problem was that when I put those flower heads in my garden, I didn't really put much thought into the location. I just stuck them in an available gap in the bed hoping a sunflower might grow there. I barely put any thought into it at all. How often do we do that in our lives? Scatter the seeds of life's potential unconsciously or haphazardly without any real consideration of the possible long-term outcome of our actions? I, for one, do it all the time.

The three sunflowers that took root the first year were fine for the first couple of months. But by the end of the season, they were leaning to one side, trying to get out from under the shade of the lacebark elm nearby. The following year there were lots of sunflower volunteers all around the area where the original three had stood, and also surprisingly far into the garden. Again, I didn't think much about where they had sprouted up, and the bigger they got, the guiltier I felt about pulling them out. So I "compromised" by thinning the weaker seedlings and allowed the five strongest to grow, two at ground zero and the other three in self-selected areas around the garden where they had landed from the hand of the wind, a bird, or a squirrel, and taken root. Do I even need to mention that the location of these three volunteers I had allowed to remain received even less attention as to appropriateness of environment? Noper. I just picked the sturdiest ones and let them stay where they lay. No consideration *and* the strongest seedlings. A dangerous combination of inattention.

The following year, and each year after that, I had huge sunflowers in all kinds of random places in my garden where I didn't want them, up to and including the front yard. And with each new, expanded reach of the unattended, unmanaged, guilt-inducing sunflowers, I was less happy and more frustrated because of my reluctance to say no and my equally irresponsible apparent inability to actually plan and then implement a plan for where I wanted those large, very focal plants.

Imagine, what if instead of seedlings allowed to run rampant in my garden, those had been life decisions? What if, instead of giant flowers I couldn't make sensible, considered choices about, it had been relationship choices? What if, instead of feeling guilty and paralyzed by a reluctance to let go of a few wildflowers, I was feeling guilty and paralyzed by a reluctance to let go of unhealthy relationships driven by childhood wounds and personal fears? Hey...wait a minute...

Looking back at my relationship with Glenn now, with a still cloudy, but more willing perspective, I can begin to see how much of this debacle was my fault. If ever there was a situation where I was trying to control an outcome I had no control over, this was it. What's interesting, of course, is that I didn't see it that way at all when the problems started. I perceived this parasitic "other woman" as a Shelob-ish outside force trying to invade my sanctuary of love. But it wasn't that simple. Things rarely are. I didn't want to see the culpability of my lover, so I targeted the outside enemy onto whom I could attach all blame. Now, mind you, a great deal of the blame actually was hers. But it wasn't all her fault, despite what I wanted to believe. However it happened, though, we all three ended up in that relationship together whether we wanted to or not, which clearly we did not. At least she and I certainly did not. Indeed, I can say (with absolute clarity about the absurdity of the statement) that I have never before been in such an intense relationship with someone I had never met. But there I was, fiercely dancing the tarantella in an effort to purge her venom from our relationship, not realizing there would never be any way to win in this twisted, toxic triangle.

Everything about this situation was bad. But one of the worst parts was the person I became when I was in it. Someone so jealous and angry, someone who was wallowing in victimhood, clingy, manipulative, and vindictive. I was operating almost exclusively from my woundedness. I became someone who was mostly unable to reach my higher perspective, and on the rare occasion when I could touch it, I couldn't hold on to it for long. I learned the hard way that when someone you love and trust lies to you repeatedly, betrays your most tender confidences, and literally sleeps with the enemy, bad things happen in your head. I could hardly believe my own behavior, and what I saw I hated. Who was this alien creature impersonating me? Instead of the calm, balanced, loving touchstone I had always been with Glenn and so many others, I basically went kind of nuts. I became paranoid and grossly insecure, filled with a depth of grief and rage so immense I could not contain, release, or process it. Of course, this only added self-loathing to the already noxious sea of negativity I was drowning in. What's even worse, these were the very characteristics that defined my nemesis whom I held in such contempt and judged so mercilessly. These flashes of white-hot reality sent me into fits of incredulity and fury with every incident. And the occasional split seconds of recognition that shot through my consciousness when I was struck by how my pot was calling her kettle black only served to enrage me more. I was in *no* mood to get all spiritual. Was she a mirror? Yep. Did I care to look at that right now? Nope. That "mirror, mirror" that was in my hand? All I wanted to do was smash that sucker across his lying, cheating face.

You know what I think? I think consciousness is a double-edged sword. I think knowing there is a higher perspective and a more loving way to view things can make it harder sometimes, because you've set the bar too high for the *really* bad times. I think being able to see yourself reflected in people, behaviors, and situations you abhor is bloody hard. And frankly, I am not sure it hastens understanding. It just paves the way. Kind of. More like a gravel path. I think awareness can be like those lousy solar-powered landscape lights. They sort of illuminate, but mostly they just vaguely point you in a dimly lit direction. And that's only if it hasn't been cloudy for very long. Then they don't work worth a damn. If you've been in the grief and rage soup for a while, those higher-consciousness solar lights are really just a tease. You're on your own, baby. Get used to it. You'll figure it out. Maybe. But it's not going to be pretty, it's not going to be easy, and it's not going to be fast. Good luck.

So here's the million-dollar question: What the hell was I doing there? What deeply held fear was holding my heart in such a totally messed up, dysfunctional situation that made my emotional life a roller coaster in a Stephen King nightmare for over two years? The answer to that question probably really wants out, but right now, I am too angry to give it oxygen. Right now, all I know is I am furious. And I'm afraid.

In this moment, I feel guilty, too. Why? Because I feel like he needs me (he says he does) and that it would break his heart if I left for good (he says it would) and he might never recover (which he says and I want to believe). But I know there is only more heartbreak in store for me if I go back, because I can no longer trust him. At the same time, I also feel trapped and afraid. Without him in my life, what would I have left? What options would I have? If I let go of this relationship, dysfunctional, toxic, and wounding though it has become, then what? Or more to the point, then who? Who else would want me now?

These thoughts of lack and scarcity are familiar within me in an ancient sort of way. Like the smell of a very old book. I really thought I had healed them, though. At least more than this. But apparently not. So, since I ignored the early handwriting on the wall two years ago, and then the wild graffiti emblazoned on the wall six months ago, now I get to be Jericho while the whole damn wall comes tumbling down on my head. Slapped upside the head with the proverbial cosmic two-by-four that demands I look at this relationship with clear, honest eyes and make a change. Right. Now. I finally managed to get unsentimental and ruthless with the sunflowers in my garden. He's next.

Here's what I know. We are all walking wounded. Yes, we can heal, and yes, sometimes the place where the wound was becomes stronger. A place where we've toughened up. But sometimes the place where the wound was remains a tender, fragile spot. A place we need to guard with love and vigilance. Sometimes the place where the wound was stays open forever, but it morphs into being open as a doorway that invites us into deeper understanding. Rumi wrote, "The wound is the place where the Light enters you." I hope he's right, because to me, the wound feels like the place where trust gushed out, and the barn door I'm slamming behind it is called Anger.

One Hundred Daffodils

Today I bought a hundred daffodils. It was a radical act of self-care. It was also an affirmation. An outward demonstration of a spiritual truth I am having trouble hanging on to right now. The truth that there is enough to go around. Enough time, enough money, enough love, enough of everything. In my particular case, I need to be reminded that there is enough love, because right now, it feels as if there is no love. None for me, anyway. At least not the kind I believed I had, in which I placed my heart and my trust, and that was so precious to me.

I would have bought more daffodils today. I wanted to. But a voice inside said no, I needed to leave enough for everyone else. As if I could make a measurable dent in the global supply of daffodils by buying too many from my little grocery store.

Driving home, I thought about what had stopped me from buying all the daffodils I wanted. After all, the whole purpose of the exercise was to soothe myself with the flowers I have loved since childhood. Distantly, I heard a faint echo within. Admonishments to not be greedy. Being scolded for wanting too much. Being punished for taking too much. Going deeper into those early memories of "not enough," I realized they were not only pervasive, but their tone was always filled with judgment and shame. "Don't take more than your fair share," "What will people think?" "Don't be so piggy," "Leave some for someone else," "You don't need those," "What is everybody else supposed to do if you take them all?" Jumping all the way over into one of Bon Bon's favorite taunts, "You'll get as fat as your other grandma if you eat all those," after she confusingly handed me an entire plate of fresh, warm sweet rolls.

As I thought about the source of these shame-laden messages of lack and their attendant dramatic consequences of greed and social ostracism, I realized what I was doing. I was globalizing my grandparents' real-life Depression era experiences of insufficiency into not only my flower buying, but into my current *love life*. The result of that weird recipe was "there is a limit to the number of available men who could love you." In fact, that number is limited to zero. Zip. The Big Egg. That guy who just repeatedly lied to you, cheated on you, and betrayed your most tender confidences? He was it. The end of the road. The last of the Mohicans. The last potential love in the known universe.

It's easy to see how living with wartime rationing could

seriously and permanently affect one's worldview. Scarcity was real back then. You could only have exactly what you needed, and often less than you needed, because there really and truly was not enough for everybody. If you took too much, someone else would suffer and maybe starve. But this is not the Great Depression. Hasn't been for three generations. And anyway, rationing never applied to available men who could love me. That connection happened in my two-year-old brain when my war-wounded grandparents hammered into me that there was not enough of anything valuable in the world. And then my father was killed.

Fear + trauma = belief.

But I know now that it's time for a reframe. As I look around the world in which I live, it's absurd to think that there is not enough of what I need, and even enough for all that I want.

Nature has always known this truth, and in my heart, I have known it too, but today I needed to be reminded. I needed some symbol of the grace of unfettered abundance to help pull me out of this nosedive of heartbreak-fed fear and scarcity.

One of my first, and still most memorable, experiences of nature's riotous abundance was with daffodils. When I was ten years old, my family moved from Rome, Italy, to Scotland as my geologist stepfather's work took him to the North Sea. My parents rented the second floor of a Regency manor house in Edinburgh, whose four floors had been sealed off from one another during the Great War in an effort to create an inconvenience sufficient enough to prevent the army from taking the house over as a base. The owners lived on the first floor, we lived on the second floor, Mrs. Fleck, the owner's mother, lived on the third floor, and the top floor, originally the servants' quarters, had been converted into offices that my stepfather and his men used.

Craiglockhart House sat on several manicured acres that swept down to a wooded dell. The dell was mysterious. It was dense and wild, so we were not allowed to venture in, but foxes and other wild creatures would sometimes venture out and into our garden. The dark, forbidden dell encircled the entire back of the estate, separated from the grounds by an ancient, decorative iron fence whose boundary was visually soft but tangibly firm, with no gate that we could ever find. My sister and I would play hide-and-seek in gigantic floral playhouses of violet and fuchsia rhododendrons, and roll down the emerald velvet lawn. But one night, when her pet rabbit was killed by a dell fox, we were reminded of the dangers just beyond the fence. This tension between wild and tame has informed my garden designs ever since we lived in Edinburgh.

Upon entering the walled grounds of Craiglockhart House, there was a sweep of garden that started at the entrance gate and followed the wall, wrapping around the front of the main house. A large fountain was focal in the center, and the entire area was enclosed by a mossy wooden rail fence designed to contain the resident flock of fifty geese who freely roamed that section of the garden most of the year. In February the geese were herded to another part of the property, and within a few weeks, the front acre, now still and quiet, began to come alive again in a different way. With the hush of nature unnoticed, small sprouts of green pushed through the ground, and up, until suddenly by March the front acre burst into a fragrant mass of floral sunshine. For a few weeks every year, thousands upon thousands, maybe even millions of daffodils rose from the earth with such density the area became virtually impassable. It was a solid sea of daffodils as far as the property stretched across the front and to the northern edge. Trumpets of vibrant yellow as loud as the geese.

Every year when the daffodils would bloom, I remember being so overcome by the immensity of their beauty that I felt it in my body. I had a physical reaction, not only to the beauty, but to the vastness of it. I had never seen so many beautiful flowers blooming anywhere in my life, appearing effortlessly from the goose-trodden mud and blooming with ferocious, unconstrained abandon. It was not just the number of daffodils, but their wildness, the fact that through no discernible intervention at all, these masses of glorious, electric blossoms pushed out of nowhere with such mad confidence, that demanded the absolute full attention of everyone who passed by. These flowers were so plural, so perfect, and so outrageously commanding it was completely impossible not to stop, captivated, mesmerized, and awed by them. Every few days for the next month, we would cut an armload or two of daffodils to put around the house, and we never put a dent in this spectacular field of gold. Standing up to my ten-year-old knees in the field of daffodils was an immersion experience of color, texture, fragrance, and magic.

So today, I bought a hundred daffodils, and tomorrow maybe I'll buy a hundred more, and the next day and the next day and the next if I want to, because daffodils remind me that there is no limit to the amount of beauty, joy, abundance, and love available in the world, to me, to you, and to everyone.

The Plane Truth

I fell in love today. I wasn't looking for love, but it found me, as love is wont to do. I was minding my own business, walking through the streets of London somewhere in Mayfair, when I happened upon Berkeley Square. I was pulled like a wood nymph into the park by the magnetism of thirty huge, seductive shade trees. As I got closer, twitterpation ensued. My breathing became shallow, my focus narrowed, and my heart began to race, all the signs of love at first sight, as I was drawn by the beautiful shedding bark and gnarled trunks of these great elders. Though I haven't studied British horticulture, judging from the mottled taupe, olive, cream, and gray shading of the bark, I was sure these trees were related to the American sycamores that I love so much. Sure enough, they were

London plane trees, a cross between American sycamores and Oriental plane trees.

Planted in 1789, the plane trees in Berkeley Square are among the oldest trees in London. It is thought that they likely self-hybridized when the two related species (*Platanus occidentalis* and *Platanus orientalis*) were planted near one another at Vauxhall Gardens during the enthusiastic years of global plant collection in the seventeenth and eighteenth centuries.

As I stood surrounded by these massive towers, I felt safe. There was something about their size and age that made me feel embraced, protected. I stood under their canopy, staring up and around for a while like a panoramic camera, taking in their vastness. I knew that underground, their roots were connected to one another, inextricably intertwined from centuries of parallel growth. I walked right up to one particularly large and knotty specimen whose undulating root flare spread wide and melted into the ground like slow flowing lava. I reached out to touch it, gently running my hand over the rough and smooth bark, lovingly, sensually, and as I did, I could feel the time held within its tissues. I stepped closer, pulled by its energy, and pressed myself against it. An exhale flowed from me as my body relaxed into the safety and support of this great mother.

It has been six months now since Glenn shattered my faith. I guess my worry about our age difference finally paid off. I should have stuck with the transition ceremony a year ago and never let him talk me into staying. But he had fought so hard to keep us together. Why would he do that?

Why would he do this? Why like this? All this suffering was so unnecessary. It didn't have to be like this. I was the one who wanted out. *He* was the one who couldn't let go. And it wasn't just the fact that he betrayed me. It was how he betrayed me, weaponizing my most fragile confidences against me. Nothing was sacred. Nothing too personal. But the cruelest was when he assured her I was no threat to her because of my age.

Leaning into the ancient plane tree and feeling its pulse against my body, I remembered a story my mother used to tell about an elderly couple she met at my grandparents' fiftieth wedding anniversary party. Struck by the grace, elegance, and pure beauty still possessed by this octogenarian, my mother turned to the woman's husband and said, "Your wife is so very beautiful."

"Yes," he replied, "her character shows on her face."

I have always wanted to age like that woman at the party, but the reality is that's just a whole lot harder in practice than it is in theory. For most of my life I frequently forgot my age and couldn't have cared less about it. But when I hit my late forties, my husband left me, and I was suddenly staring down the barrel of starting all over again, I got downright weird about my age. I was embarrassed by it in a way. Mostly, I was afraid of it. Fortunate to look younger than my years, I stopped telling my age, and if anyone pressed, I would lie. I'll tell you what, though, there is something strangely liberating about having the secrets you keep and your greatest fears used against you. Once they're out there, all the psychic energy you were using to keep that stuff under wraps, those fears and secrets that were sucking your spirit dry like a surgically inserted mind leech, they're all suddenly lifted. You can rail against it all you want. You can hate the betrayer, you can hate the "other woman," you can hate the circumstances, and you can hate the truth, but the fact remains, the secret is no longer secret. Surrender is your only option. Surrender, and acceptance. Of course, that kind of forced surrender doesn't feel the same as the kind of surrender that comes with enlightenment, that's for sure. But nevertheless, you are free. Free from the bondage of your self-imposed shame.

Melting into the giant tree that supported my wounded weight that day in Berkeley Square, both intoxicated and sobered by its power and beauty, I realized this stunning majesty, this breathtaking beauty, this awe-inspiring arboreal goddess was not beautiful in spite of her age, but because of it.

I decided in that moment that Glenn's cutting words could only hurt me if I believed them to be true. I understood his actions stemmed from his own emotional weakness, and I could take what he said personally...or not. For the first time since I'd read his words and lost my faith not only in him, but in myself, I realized that the riverbank I had been clinging to, fighting to hang on through the torrential, rushing, garbage-laden floodwaters of my life—that riverbank was never my salvation.

Over the course of my life, I have said no a thousand times in a hundred different ways to stepping into my autonomy, believing in my value, and standing in my power.

But I realize what I had been struggling against all along was the flow of my own life. I finally understood that by holding on to the edge, I was holding on to the past. Muddy waters, garbage and all, it was *my life* I was resisting. So I released my grip and let myself flow into the River of Yes.

When I'm gone, I want people to say, "She wore her age like the patina on sparkling copper, more beautiful for the time that had passed and the life she led. She had the kind of rarefied beauty that can only come with age. A deep beauty borne of wisdom, compassion, and a life fully lived, and she carried with grace and dignity."

Like a tree. Like a tree in Berkeley Square. Like a London plane tree.

Deep Trust

My philosophy is to let nature's balance find its way in my garden. This philosophy began with the purchase of my first home a few years after I graduated from college. Truth be told, it was less a philosophy at that point and more a lack of knowledge to the contrary with a supporting lack of focus on the garden. The house was a pretty English Tudor cottage built in the 1920s, untouched and "unruined" by insensitive updating, so my initial interest was in the loving restoration of this beautiful home. That meant the garden took a back seat for the first year or so, which allowed me to live through a full year of observation and find out what was already growing there, a serendipitous accident of available time, which turned out to be most fortunate.

Once I began to address the garden, I quickly realized that there was a tremendous amount of information about gardening that I did not possess. All of it, in fact. I knew nothing about gardening or how to manage and treat a garden, and much of the available information at the time had to do with what chemicals to apply when, to make this grow or that die. I found the whole thing enormously confusing and honestly, kind of creepy. And yet, since this was the practice of the day, I set out to learn. But you know what? I never could. Not because I was incapable of learning the information, but because every time I tried to apply what I was learning about which noxious chemical to use to eradicate some fungus or caterpillar or weed in my garden, I felt a huge internal resistance. It just seemed completely counterintuitive to put poison on my garden, and I didn't want to do it.

It was then that I began to learn about the natural way of gardening. "Organic gardening" as it was called, the absurdity of the name being almost too on the nose to be believed. Nevertheless, in the early 1980s, "organic" gardening was perceived as exotic and quite fringe. It's funny now to reflect on those days when I would speak to garden clubs about organic gardening and no one had ever heard of it. Everyone considered me so "earthy" as I talked about the natural ways to control pests and diseases, and gave recipes for garden treatments using Ivory dishwashing liquid and dough balls because there were no natural controls, or even low impact treatments that could be bought ready-made. And I got so into it! It was fun and exciting for me to discover ways to live more in tune with nature. I was growing and cooking with fresh herbs when they had to be mail ordered, and prepared homemade bath and body treatments. I was cooking with flowers and flower essences when I knew of no one else who was doing those things. Years later when she became famous, friends joked that I was Martha Stewart before she was.

What was more interesting to me than the actual treatment methods, though, was the underlying philosophy of organic gardening. In a word, it's about trust. In two words, it's about deep trust. In four words, it's about deep trust and release. Because allowing nature to handle the garden demands deep trust in nature's process and a willingness to allow things to be out of our control. It means trusting that all is as it should be. Trusting that there is greater wisdom in a single blade of grass than we shall ever possess. It also means allowing, releasing, letting go of our need to organize, systemize, and have our way. It means gardening as a teacher. Gardening as a personal process. Gardening as a spiritual practice.

I've spent a lot of time over the last fifteen years working on the concepts of releasing attachment and the need for control in my life. Initially these ideas were completely foreign to me and, frankly, distasteful. In my world, love was shown by the degree to which one fuses with the other, including people, places, events, and things. But gardening with deep trust means understanding that you do not now, never have had, and never will have control. Any thoughts to the contrary are illusions. Deep trust means releasing the need to be in control of anything, let alone everything.

Gardening with deep trust means realizing that the very act of gardening is an effort to change the natural order of things. I once read a line that said, "A gardener is one who fights with nature." When I read that, I found it jarring. That was in no way how I viewed myself as a gardener. Quite the contrary. I was Gaia. Nature Girl. I was one with the garden. And yet deep down, I understood the truth in the statement. Gardening is an act of dominance, an act of force that requires constant vigilance. Maybe I was one with the garden, but I was not one with nature. Not as long as I was trying to control it. So what does that say about me?

I think it says I am learning to let go and trust, but I am still a novice. In many aspects of my life, I have been actively resistant to forcing. Indeed, in the gardening realm, "forcing" bulbs in winter was something I was never drawn to. It felt weirdly aggressive to me, and the plants it produced always looked somehow deformed. Sometimes only a little but sometimes grotesquely so. They were either too leggy or stunted, bent one way or the other, straining for light, with sparse or weak foliage and puny blooms. Forcing bulbs always seemed like a monument to impatience. A resistance to being here and now. Wanting "this" to be over, or worse, pretending that "this" isn't even the current reality. Like teenagers wanting to grow up too fast, forcing is being unwilling to wait for life to unfold. Grandma used to tell me all the time, "Darling, don't wish your life away," to which I am sure I rolled my eyes. But now I understand. To everything there is a season, and I trust that. I trust that deeply.

To Sit in Solemn Silence

I have very sensitive senses, and I often find the sounds of the city to be stressful. Traffic, sirens, cell phones, leaf blowers, and even the constant chatter of people can make me tired and want to cocoon. Conversely, the sound of the breeze rustling in the trees, of storms rumbling in the distance, the tapping of rainfall are soothing to me, and even more, the gift of silence.

Silence is something we don't often have exposure to in our day-to-day lives. When we are out in the world, it's rare for a person to hear nothing at all, or only the sounds of their own making. Even farmers do little anymore without the hum of machinery around them. This constant noise, this pervasive onslaught of sound, is detrimental to our souls. To my soul, at least. And I long for a refuge where I can remove myself from it.

The other night I had a dream. I got into a boat and started out to sea. I wanted to get away. I considered just motoring out for an hour or so, then coming back to shore. But I also considered going to the Bahamas. In my dream, my friend Mary was suddenly there with me.

"Where are you going?" she asked.

"I don't know. Maybe the Bahamas. Wanna go?"

"Sure!" she said. And off we went.

When we got to the Bahamas, we found a festive, tropical party atmosphere, which was not what I had hoped for. We went up to our rooms and changed, and as we were heading out to the beach, Mary and some other women who had joined us out of nowhere (as people in dreams tend to do) began to run through the rooms of the hotel, dodging furniture and weaving in and out between hotel guests. I was last in the line, and reluctant to be running through the hotel for no apparent reason. Some older friends from church waved from across the room. I returned the greeting with some surprise, and when I turned back to my group, I realized I had lost them. I felt the sudden pierce of childhood pain. You know the one—being left out, forgotten, lost but not missed. Integrating that sad, familiar pang with the simultaneous relief of not having to go to the beach party, I turned and went out to the pool instead. I jumped in and swam down to the bottom of the deep end, and there, I lay down. It was beautiful. Very deep, very quiet, and very blue. As I lay on the bottom of the pool, I remember being distracted by the question of why I was not floating back up to the top. I never questioned how I was breathing, but this wonder about how I could just lie there on the bottom of the deep end of the pool without floating up to the surface would not leave me alone. I remember being annoyed that I could not just relax and enjoy it. But the question was incessant. To try to understand, I swam back to the top and then back down. Again I lay down, and again I easily settled on the bottom of the deep end of the pool, comfortably but curiously stable and weighted.

In addition to more obscure messages, I believe this dream was a cry from my subconscious to find a place of peace, and to go there. Preferably for good. Somewhere like the house I rented outside of Taos, tucked away on the mesa across from the sacred mountains, where I could go out at night and hear nothing but the occasional distant cries of coyotes and the soft pull of the wind. Or the place I rented in New Zealand, perched high on the edge of a bluff, where the sound of the crashing waves a hundred feet below were muffled to a soft, soothing, rhythmic hum, and whose walls were massive glass doors on three sides which, when opened in full, created a giant decompression chamber where nature rushed in to touch my skin and fill my every breath with the peace that comes from a deep connection to the One.

At home, when I first open my eyes in the morning, I look out the glass doors of my bedroom and see green. Tousled, gangly, unruly green. I have no fewer than eleven volunteer trees in my garden, some of which I allowed to grow where they sprouted and others I moved as saplings to a vaguely more suitable place. Even so, all of them are still a little unmanaged in terms of placement. But I confess, I kind of love that about them. Those brazen uninviteds remind me that the best laid plans of mice and men don't factor in nature's tenacity. And they remind me that nature always plays the last card, which is comforting, especially in these times.

My garden has a number of designed elements, but because I have so little time to spend on it, it has developed a style and personality of its own. Walking through my garden, I must push aside overly enthusiastic spirea that have now completely blocked two walkways which were always a little too narrow, lift the low-hanging tendrils of wisteria gone rogue, and duck to pass under vitex branches that I can't bring myself to prune any higher. I left an opening in my front hedge screen of Japanese ligustrum and laid a bluestone path through the garden to my door in an attempt to make it easier for guests to get in, but right away, a gigantic sunflower sprouted at the gateway, blocking the opening like an overzealous bodyguard, so I guess that entrance is closed, at least until autumn. On the west side, there is a pear tree I found as a three-inch sapling under the split halves of my grand, old Bradford that was mortally cleaved by a microburst from a fast-moving storm. I saved that little baby, and it is a beautiful, perfectly branched nine-foot-tall teenager now, erect and healthy, just eight months later. I absolutely love that little tree. But I never would have bought it. It's like an adorable puppy who just showed up at my door and I kept, even though I didn't really want another dog. And there's the Chinese tallow tree I found as a tiny two-inch sapling in a client's alley. It was in an old black plastic nursery pot that had filled with leaf debris over time and accepted this seed from the neighboring giant. Somehow, I end up loving these trees more than the perfectly formed and painstakingly selected ones I buy from nurseries and growers. It's not fair, I know. All those impeccably balanced, symmetrical trees are lovely and deserve my devotion as well, but these awkward, bendy, often misshapen, unruly children have a charm so distinctly their own, I cannot resist favoring them for their raw authenticity and free spirits. I have no inclination whatsoever to try to straighten them or prune them into conformity, or otherwise right their rebel souls. Those beautiful, low-hanging, contorted Chinese tallow branches that are currently scraping the front drive and my crotchety neighbor's last nerve—those are the exact branches that give her interest and grace, and they will give her romance and majesty when she's all grown up. They are what give her character. Strong, independent, unique character. And isn't that the most important quality we can cultivate in those with whose lives we are entrusted?

For years I spent many quiet hours in my garden, sitting, thinking, walking around, noticing, communing. I usually went out each morning for tea and a peaceful transition into the day. But a few years ago, the city expanded a nearby highway and added underground express lanes. When they began the expansion, they cut down hundreds of mature trees along the length of the construction site, over seventy of which flanked the edges of the old highway in the mile between the two major cross streets where I live. Seventy huge trees, many of them live oaks, some cottonwoods, sycamores, red oaks, hackberries, and others. Those trees acted as a powerful sound barrier at my house. Before the highway expansion I couldn't hear the highway in my garden at all, but now I can, and I hate that. Depending on the direction of the wind, it can be more or less noticeable, but the fact that I can ever hear it bothers me. So now, I spend more time inside my house looking out at my garden than I do actually in it, and for me that is a terrible loss.

I have plans to move somewhere private and undeveloped enough that I can retreat to a sanctuary of silence whenever I am home. But for now, I shall continue to encourage arboreal volunteers as a buffer, and add water features with sounds that melt together with the city's voice to create a softer song and a kinder, more nurturing haven of tranquility amidst the tumult around me. And I shall continue to seek peace from within.

Chapter 5

Florescence

No Need for
Validation

I have an addiction. A serious, debilitating addiction. Not
to a substance. No, this is something different. My addiction is invisible. Its source is not illegal or even controlled.
For the most part, it isn't even looked down upon in society
because most people never notice it's there. My addiction
is so easy to hide that people become willing accomplices
without ever having a clue that they are participating in
feeding my crippling obsession. They don't know because
their participation is not only voluntary but usually quite
enthusiastic. They feel great about themselves afterward and
great about me. Unlike an enabler who passes a crack pipe
to a junkie or a drink to an alcoholic knowing they have
a problem, the participants in my addiction leave thinking
they have uplifted me and have been loving, supportive, and

kind. They have no idea as they shower me with praise that I am addicted to external validation.

But how could they know? I'm a master at my methods of seeking that fix. I am a meticulous perfectionist and a dedicated overachiever who makes sure my work is good enough that people are more than happy to say so in the most effusive and exuberant ways. Do I want that to stop? No. Not even a little bit. It is nice to be appreciated, and people enjoy sharing how the work or presence of others has helped them, or affected their lives in a positive way. But what I *do* want to stop is my need for it. It's not so much a problem in my work, though it certainly exists there. It is in my relationships that this addiction is unmanageable. Absolutely, completely, and paralyzingly unmanageable.

I find myself at this place in my life, divorced after decades of marriage and another near decade of separation, and instead of being footloose and fancy free, I am a huddled mess of attachment to my relationship with Glenn.

Glenn's love was soul food, absolutely. But now that relationship has ended, and I am a basket case. Why? Because the grounded confidence and self-assurance I thought I had been building and reclaiming over the years with him has collapsed like a cardboard fort. Without my awareness, the love, attraction, and admiration Glenn felt for me was the foundation on which my personal healing was being built. I didn't learn through Glenn's love that I was attractive, had value, and was worthy; I felt worthy, attractive, and valuable *because* of Glenn's love. And now that it's gone, I suddenly realize I have frighteningly little personal foundation or sense of my own value at all. And that which I do have at this moment is so faint, so tenuous, I can barely feel or summon it.

As I contemplate this worrying fact, I begin to consider my surroundings. In my garden at home there are crape myrtles covered in blossoms, crimson Chinese pistachio trees, wildly abundant blue asters blooming, and cadmium yellow cottonwoods shimmering and rustling in the breeze. And here, in my mountain hideaway in New Mexico, even though I am in the high desert, there is nothing desolate about this place. Everywhere I look there are miles of fragrant sagebrush and waves of the willowy reeds for which this area was named standing bare against the landscape, yet vibrant and shimmering red before the mountain backdrop. And the sky here, a legendary kaleidoscope of constantly changing colors so stunning one can hardly drive down a road of any size during sunrise or sunset hours without seeing cars pulled to the side, full of people whose lives are not so pressing they cannot afford a few minutes to stop and appreciate the magnificence of this world.

Scanning the beauty that surrounds me, I am struck by how independent nature is. Absolutely, completely, and utterly independent. How I long for that. I expect it would surprise no one to learn that every New Year for the past nine years I have included *independence* on my list of things I wanted to create for myself in the coming year. Truth be told, I thought I was doing that wrapped in the warmth, constant reassurance, and support of Glenn's love. But now I see what independence really looks like. Independence means standing, unwavering, in the full expression of your beauty, your purpose, and your value, no matter what the surrounding conditions might be. It means living full on, unrestrained, out loud, at maximum capacity, not because someone tells you how great you are, but simply because you exist. It means taking ownership of who you are to such a degree that nothing and no one can devalue you by their opinion. They cannot inflate you with the giving of their love nor diminish you by withdrawing it. It means knowing you are worthy, unique, and lovable no matter what anyone else thinks. Independence—real independence—means flourishing without the need for validation.

One might assume that as a landscape designer, I am constantly working in my garden, but the truth is I do basically nothing in my garden anymore except mulch in the fall (usually) and water in the summer. Every huge, glorious, colorful, fragrant, outrageously beautiful plant in my garden is pretty much doing its thing all by itself with little or no reliance on me and certainly without any need for me to tell it how great it is. Nature needs no emotional support from me or anybody else. Mind you, it gets it anyway. In the world of people giving what they want to receive, I am out there all the time telling my garden how beautiful it is, but I know this is not why my garden grows. My garden grows because it is completely and totally immersed in the experience of being alive, and it is growing and thriving and expressing itself for that simple reason. It is alive and therefore worthy. It is alive and therefore glorious. It is alive and therefore complete.

What would that feel like? To be so sure of one's own value and self-worth that every day it was the most natural thing in the world to show up in all one's greatness and glory, shining for all the world to see with no agenda, nothing to prove, nothing to overcome, nothing to heal, and no one to please. Imagine what would be possible if every drop of energy we had could be used to bring our gifts to the world, and no energy was wasted on seeking the admiration and approbation of others. What if virtue, accomplishment, productivity, and right action really were sufficiently their own reward, and we naturally expressed them with ease and grace.

The need for external validation is insidious. It robs us of our self-trust and deadens our personal barometer—that perfect internal guidance system that tells us what will bring us joy and how we should be living our own lives. The need for external validation makes us question our own instincts and gives our power to others who can (and do) easily use the withholding of validation as a weapon to control us and make us do what they want, what they think is best for us, or keep us in "our place." What would we be without external validation? We would be independent, and independently able to express ourselves, purely and honestly as ourselves, exactly as it feels authentic. Self-expression is our natural state. Reliance on the opinion of others is crippling and antithetical to our perfect God-given design.

I remember a friend telling a story when our children were babies about her sister whose daughter was, at that time, a toddler. Active and all over the place as toddlers are, if this child was awake, she was exploring her world and trying new skills. One day, my friend was at her sister's house and they were chatting as the little girl amused herself at their feet. At one point, the child discovered she could take apart a simple toy and put it back together. Her mother and my friend were deep in conversation and only peripherally aware of what the child was doing. After taking it apart and putting it back together a few times unnoticed and unacknowledged, the child called out for her mother's attention. The mother and my friend responded to the child as she proceeded to demonstrate her new skill. Since the mother and her sister were otherwise occupied, the mother said something along the lines of "That's nice, honey." The child looked disappointed, and called to her mother again to watch. She replayed her new trick, and the mother again said, "Mmm-hmm, that's good," at which point the child scowled and said, "More yay!"

On one hand, this can be viewed as just another cute kid story, but on the other hand, it is a cautionary tale. When we raise our children to think every minor accomplishment they achieve is "Yay!" worthy, we set them up for disappointment and false, unhealthy, even absurd expectations of what awaits them when they get out into the real world. We may think we are building their self-esteem, but what we are actually doing is robbing them of the inherent pleasure and sense of fulfillment that comes with the simple act of accomplishment.

An example of this came when I lent a sizable amount of money to a friend who had a pattern of being financially irresponsible. When the woman (who was in her forties at the time) did eventually repay me, I thanked her, but she was clearly bothered when I just acknowledged receipt and was about to move on to a different subject. She interrupted me so she could point out the obvious to me again—that she had paid back the money in full. I thanked her again, but she held my attention with palpable exasperation, and with a tone of one who was a little offended, she informed me of my faux pas, instructing me that my thanks was not equal to her gesture. She felt she deserved some level of praise. Bemused and more than a little annoyed myself at this point, I had to tell her with as much kindness as I could muster, "You know, you don't get a gold star for meeting the minimum requirements."

In addition to setting children up for an unhealthy validation-driven worldview, we inadvertently teach them that unless they get their yay, somehow their accomplishment was not good enough, not worthy enough to command our praise, and therefore it must not be worthwhile at all. The opposite extreme can also be true. I was certainly not raised in a house full of yays, and insufficient yays can also lead to a pathological need for validation, but ultimately, no matter how we were raised, it is our responsibility to find the yay within us.

As I observe the partial but significant erosion of self-esteem I feel from the end of my relationship with Glenn, I can see how I placed too much of the weight of responsibility for my self-image on the perilously sandy foundation of love and validation from another... again. This is exactly what I did with Daniel. That being said, I also understand that at the end of my marriage, I was so emotionally incapacitated it is unlikely I could have summoned the internal fortitude necessary to expand into my independence unaided. I needed Glenn, exactly the way he showed up, to help me build the tender new roots of personal strength. I needed his gentle support, unfettered adoration, and absolute belief in me at a time when I could not believe in myself. But now, it is time for me to graduate to a higher, more self-sufficient place. A place where the loss of his yay does not send me into a tailspin of self-doubt and depression. A place where the only yay that matters is the one that comes to me from my own heart. The place where all yays must originate—in the personal experience of grace in our own lives.

The Giving Tree

I have trust issues. I guess it shouldn't be surprising that I have trust issues. Given the course of my life so far, if I didn't have trust issues today, it could only be because I had been sleepwalking through the last five and a half decades. And maybe I was sleepwalking through the first thirty years or so, but I feel pretty awake now. I mean, clearly, I am not fully awake. I think that's called enlightenment, and I have a long way to go before I start levitating. But at least now, I notice when I am projecting, I know many of the ways in which my wounds outwardly express themselves, and I have developed enough humility to (mostly) realize my judgments are never about the other person. I can hear myself now when I am speaking from my wounded spirit, and if I don't hear myself right away, I can at least recognize the truth when a trusted friend points it out to me.

Like last night. I was reading Mary Pipher's *Seeking Peace: Chronicles of the Worst Buddhist in the World*. At one point she was talking about her husband and, to paraphrase, said one of the things she loved about him was how steady he was. And then she said, "I know he will never leave me." My immediate reaction (and it was a *reaction*) was "Ha! That's what *you* think! There's no such thing as a man who would never leave."

Wow. Wounded much?

When I had that reaction, I froze. I slowly closed the book, and then my eyes, and I asked myself, "Do you really believe that?"

I answered, "Yes."

Then I asked, "But is it really true?"

And I answered, "I don't know...I mean, it has been true for me."

"But is it really true?"

What I did next was scroll through all the evidence I could think of that supported the truth of my belief. A horror show of every example I could muster that proved my thesis. Everything from my own experiences to those of my friends, and those of complete strangers onto whom I overlaid my belief with appalling assumptions made out of whole cloth. Or, more accurately, made out of cloth that was anything but whole. Cloth that was fragmented, fractured, filthy, and frayed. A veritable patchwork quilt of broken vows, broken dreams, broken connections, and broken trust woven together into my broken heart, broken spirit, and broken worldview. It was evidence all right, but not of my thesis. It was evidence of how utterly decimated my ability to trust had become after a lifetime of being abandoned and betrayed.

After Glenn's epic final betrayal, I remember saying to anyone who would listen, "I have no idea how to handle this. I've never been betrayed before." I'm sure everyone who had known me well over the years mentally cocked their heads and thought, "Uhhh...really? You sure about that?"

At the time I was sure. I was sure because I couldn't see my forest for my own trees. Over the course of the next two years, with the loving guidance of Dr. Barbara Graham, I discovered that abandonment and betrayal were the two most prevalent recurring themes in my life. It started with the death of my father, developed through the cruelty of Bon Bon, and solidified through my mother's well-meaning but radically wrong decision to continue to allow Bon Bon to be in my life. These early episodes of abandonment and betrayal set the stage for me to replicate those experiences over and over and over again, in virtually every important relationship of my life. Betrayal and abandonment were so normalized in my experience that I didn't even know they were there. I had no personal set point for what a healthy relationship looked like. Zero. It wasn't until the betrayal by Glenn, my most trusted lover, that I was jolted out of my habituated relationship practices and catapulted headlong into yet another dark night of the soul, which became a state of exploration leading in the direction of understanding. Turns out, Glenn was my red pill.

Some people believe in a thing called soul contracts. An agreement of sorts with other souls who love us so much they are willing to be the teachers in life for the lessons our souls most want and need to learn. An agreement, in some cases, to be "the bad guy" so that we have the opportunity to figure out how to heal. I have no idea if that's true, but here's what I do know: Glenn loved me enough to be that for me. He was young, impatient, foolish, and lacked self-control, but Glenn loved me enough on a soul level to sacrifice himself in my eyes—to have me hate him if necessary—that I might move into a higher state of consciousness. Of course, if I did manage to use his facilitation to come to a deeper level of understanding and therefore a higher level of consciousness, then in cosmic theory, I would no longer hate him. I would be grateful to him. Nice and tidy. And isn't that exactly how love is supposed to work? To keep lifting us higher and higher? If there is such a thing as an eternal soul, I don't think its job is to just sit around and wait to be delivered. I think we're expected to do most of the work ourselves, at least to the best of our abilities. Love is at the root of every world religion. Love is at the root of all creation. It is love that never fails. I had lived my whole life seeking love, but I didn't know what love really even looked like. And I'm just going to go out on a limb here and say the chances of finding something with no idea of what it looks like is a long shot at best. But our love was real. It was my love for Glenn and his for me that ultimately opened a portal to a path to a clue to the mystery of the secret of real love so I could at least get an idea of what it might look like. And it was the loss of that love that forced me to take my first tentative steps toward discovering the source of my suffering. Not the cause. Not the circumstances that led to it. The actual source.

When Alex was little, I read to him every night. One of the books that came highly recommended was called *The Giving Tree* by Shel Silverstein. It was considered a classic, so I didn't read it first before reading it to him. Big mistake. At the beginning, it was fine.

"Once there was a tree ... and she loved a little boy."

So far so good. Me too.

"And the boy loved the tree ... very much. And the tree was happy."

Okay, I could relate to this. But the further I read, the more I hesitated. This was going downhill pretty fast. This little boy is kind of a jerk. Surely this is going to get better ...

But it didn't get better. It got worse. By the end of the book, I was crying and I hated that kid. I hated that kid, and I hated that book. I felt devastated. When I finished it, I declared, "Well, that was horrible," which I'm sure puzzled poor little Alex. I was so upset I never read it to him again. But I kept the book. Every once in a while, I would pick it up and flip through. Yep. I still hate this book. That boy was a jackass. And seriously, Tree, you're an

idiot. Codependent much? Good Lord. How are you supposed to survive if you let him cut you all the way down
to the ground? Have you no sense at all? This is so stupid.
Ugh.

Every time I looked at that book, it made me mad. And
yet, I kept it.

In the major relationships of my life, I had done everything
I thought I was supposed to do. I had adored Daniel and
built my world around him. I wanted nothing but to make
him happy and see him be successful. That didn't work out
too well for me, so when Glenn came along, I experimented
with being adored. I wasn't very good at receiving, but I got
better at it. I liked it. It felt good. I certainly preferred it to
the other way. But in the end, that didn't work out too well
for me either. There was something I still was not getting.
Something I continued to do wrong. There was something
I couldn't see as I wandered through the forest of my own
trees. I knew it was there. I could sense it. I just couldn't
find it.

While I was working through my swan dive of despair
with Barbara, she often gave me suggestions for ways I
could be kinder to myself and my body. But they all
seemed tremendously self-indulgent and kind of silly to
me, so I never even tried a single one. I spent week after
week, month after month, year after year trying to understand why the circumstances of my life were what they
were. I was always in my head. How could I have so mis-
managed my life that I would find myself here in my

fifties, alone and emotionally desolate with no clue what I had done to get here, so I could at least try to fix it. Over time, despair turned into frustration, and frustration turned into anger.

Once Anger moved in this time, it set up housekeeping.

Break Up, Break Down, Break Through

I had been working for years through therapy to process my life and especially my impending divorce, which was why I was in such a good place around the closure of my marriage by the time it happened. But since I had been so blindsided by Glenn's betrayal just three weeks after my divorce was final, my sessions with Barbara had gotten way more intense than before. I was experiencing rage so immense I felt changed at a cellular level. I was angry all the time. At everyone. Glenn's treachery was so unexpected, so unnecessary, and so absolute that incredulity possessed me.

Grief-fed fury penetrated everything I did, everyone I interacted with, and every thought I had. It blew out in microbursts on an almost daily basis. If depression is anger turned inward, then my years of depression were proof that I had a lifetime of unexpressed anger that had just been given a blowhole. All those years I thought I was being so civilized. I judged all the couples I knew who fought with each other. I thought they were being so uncivilized. I considered myself to be an exceedingly polite person. Indeed, I was so polite, I was oblivious to my actual feelings. But now, back up, baby. I was the pressure cooker you didn't want to be in the same room with. I was emotionally out of control. I was Carrie at Homecoming.

Shortly after my blowup with Glenn, my son, Alexander, asked his beloved to marry him. One of my greatest regrets is that I was not able to be more emotionally available to them during that time of joy. I didn't know whether I was transforming for the better or changing for the worse, but the old me was definitely gone. I was disintegrating. Literally *dis*-integrating the framework of my being. Unlearning what I had always thought was true. I was the caterpillar who was liquefying. My head was popping off. All I could do was hope I didn't emerge as some lame-ass pantry moth who would fly straight into one of my scented candles when I got out. That would be just perfect. Emerge, incinerate, fall into melted wax, and live out eternity as Madame Tussauds monument to doing it wrong.

Alex and Lacey's engagement lasted two years. Unfortunately, it coincided exactly with two of the worst years of my life. I tried dozens of processes to "move the anger through," but Anger was having none of it. I was stuck in a feedback loop of grief, rage, and regret. I built an effigy in my garage that I took to with a plastic baseball bat. When that felt unsatisfying, I took to it with an old wooden tennis racket. When that didn't help, I finally went after it with a massive ten-inch, industrial iron screwdriver and tore it to shreds while I muffled my screams with blaring metal music so the neighbors wouldn't call the police. I shredded and rebuilt it over and over as I screamed and cried, until I finally broke. When I broke, I broke *down.* I collapsed onto the concrete floor sobbing, wailing, keening for hours and hours. I couldn't stop. I could barely breathe. I was out of my body. All I could see was a vast, infinite black tunnel that I was falling into.

I don't know how long I lay there in hysterics, but it was a long time. So long that, after a few hours, I began to despair that I would ever be able to pull myself back. In a momentary crack in the darkness, when my body was so racked it stilled for survival, I managed to drag myself into my house and onto my bed. No sooner was I there than the convulsive lamentations returned, and I lay there for goodness knows how much longer, purging the tears that had built up inside me for decades, cursing an unfair world. As I fell deeper and deeper into the abyss, my fear of no return pushed me to reach for my phone, and in sporadic moments of breath, I sent a text to everyone I knew who prayed, and asked for help. Most sent back encouraging words, but my friend Chris, who has some experience with emergencies, recognized this was not your everyday prayer request and immediately responded to it as the emergency it was, with usable, practical solutions.

"Can you walk into the kitchen?"

"I think so."

"Eat something. Food is grounding."

"Okay." I ate three bites of a banana.

"Did you eat something?"

"Yes."

"Now go get in the pool. It will shift your focus and soothe your energy."

I walked outside like someone in a trance. I put down the phone and stepped into the pool, fully clothed, and waded into the deepest water. The rush of cool water against my emotionally overheated skin brought me back into connection with my body, and I began to reinhabit myself.

After a while, I heard a text come in.

"You gonna be okay now?"

"I think so. Thank you."

"Call me when you can."

"I will."

When I got out of the water, I went inside and slept for the rest of the day. The next day, I felt like I had been in a train wreck. I naively hoped this would be a turning point in my anger, but it wasn't. It was just one step closer to... who knows where. Somewhere that isn't here.

After Alex and Lacey married, they decided to move to New Zealand for a year, so within six weeks, they had packed up all their worldly belongings, sold Lacey's car, drove Alex's car here from LA, and took off for a yearlong adventure on the other side of the world. I missed him, and was still having a terribly hard time myself. I didn't want to spend an entire Christmas without seeing my son, so I decided to go to him. I had wanted to visit New Zealand ever since I was in college, long before the Lord of the Rings made it the destination du jour. Since it's about as far away as you can go and still be on this planet, I wanted to give myself time to get to know it, so I made plans to spend the month of December there. Alex and Lacey were covering as much territory as they could while they were in New Zealand, so they helped me create an itinerary of places they had already been, and we agreed I would spend most of my time visiting their "must see" places on my own. We planned to meet at the beginning for a few days when I arrived and then again at the end of the month for Christmas and my birthday. About a week into my trip, we met in Queenstown. Alex suggested he and I take the gondola up the mountain alone to see the view. While we were riding up the mountainside, he said, "Mom, I need to ask you something."

"Okay."

"I know you've been through a really hard time. And I love you and want to support you. But I need to know . . . is this . . . anger"—he hesitated—"the new normal?"

I let his question settle in. "I don't know," I said in all honesty.

"I mean, I can handle whatever I need to. I'd just like to know if you think this will pass."

"I'm sorry, honey. I want it to, but I just don't know."

It was a brief but thoroughly heartbreaking conversation. The thought of Alex feeling as if he needed to create some kind of protective distance between us was about the worst thing I could imagine in the world. And yet, it was out of my control. I was at the mercy of my internal workings. I was doing everything I knew how to do. I couldn't make myself heal any faster. I could only surrender to my soul's timing and pray I didn't lose my son in the process.

I had flown into Auckland, then taken another short flight to Christchurch on the South Island and rented a car. This alone represented a feat of immense courage on my part. I had never been so far away by myself, and I had never driven in a country where you drive on the wrong side of the road *and* the wrong side of the car. Furthermore, my particular brand of learning difference makes maps virtually useless for me. I look at a map and see chaos. So I had to use the GPS on my phone, but wireless service is not altogether reliable in New Zealand. Plus, you think you're going somewhere they speak English, and you are, but it's kind of like going to Scotland, Ireland, or Wales. They speak English there, too, but the street signs have a lot of incomprehensible words. In Scotland and Ireland, they're in Gaelic. In Wales, they're in Welsh. In New Zealand, they're in Maori. Take these things together with the fact that nearly every intersection in New Zealand is a dizzying roundabout, and I promise you, it was a major challenge to both drive and navigate the entire South Island and then the North Island on my own.

That being said, New Zealand for me was paradise. It was paradise for a lot of reasons, not the least of which is that there are only about 4.5 million people in the entire country, and over 1.5 million of them live in Auckland.

That leaves only about 3 million people inhabiting the entire rest of the country, or around *half a million fewer* people than live in *Montreal*. In other words, New Zealand is an introvert's dream come true. I was there when the lupines were blooming around Lake Tekapo. Standing in a field with millions of chest-high flowers in shades of all my favorite colors, every breath filled with their intoxicating fragrance, was a spiritual experience. Indeed, almost everything about New Zealand was a spiritual experience for me. It was a horticultural haven with a stunning lack of humanity—and by humanity, I mean humans—which was exactly what I needed. A bucolic sanctuary with miles and miles and miles of green and not a single billboard. A retreat from the relentless, subliminally screaming input of home, where every square inch of printable space is an opportunity to sell you something you don't need, shower you with unsettling political news, or remind you that you're too fat. A place where I could get a perfect to-go cup of English tea with milk at any gas station. That alone was heaven for me. I slept when I wanted, ate when I wanted, drove when I wanted, and stopped when I wanted. I only did what I wanted every day for weeks. I found secret, private beaches I had entirely to myself. I was alone in the best, most beautiful way imaginable. No one but Alex ever called because everyone back home knew I was incommunicado. Same with email. I had an away message that said I would have little access to the internet, and I'd respond when I got back. I was free. Free. *Free*.

I don't know what happened to me when I was in New

Zealand. I didn't feel it happen. I didn't feel anything except peace and tranquility for weeks. Looking back on it, I guess it was like what Joan Rivers said: "I wish I could tell you it gets better. But it doesn't get better. You get better." And I did. Somehow, I got better. I honestly wasn't even trying to get better by that point. I had surrendered to the process. But somewhere along the miles of blue highways, the hillsides covered in sheep, the waves crashing against unmolested shores, and the fields of fragrant flowers, I got better.

When I arrived at the house we had rented for Christmas in Whangarei, and walked in the door, Alex looked at me, tilted his head, and said, "What happened?"

"I don't know."

Then he smiled and said, "Welcome back."

Cottonwood Chorus

There is a cottonwood tree in my neighbor's backyard a couple of doors down. Towering over a hundred feet high, at least thirty feet taller than the surrounding trees, it is the matriarch of the neighborhood. There are a lot of things I love about this tree, but the thing I love most is the sound it makes. It's a very distinctive sound, louder and crisper than the rustle of most trees. The sound is almost a soft clicking, but prettier than that. More like raindrops falling on a skylight or a babbling brook nearby. I can hear it clearly in my garden over a football field's distance away. When the cottonwood sings, it is almost always a harbinger of something good. Usually a storm or a cold front.

A couple of years ago, I had a tiny volunteer sapling in my garden, no more than two inches high. I wasn't sure what it was, but since it had sprouted directly under the drip line of the Bradford pear tree that had recently died after splitting in a storm, and the leaves were similar, I assumed it was her offspring. The little tree grew quickly—very quickly. Probably too quickly for a pear tree, I thought, when I thought about it, which was hardly ever. A couple of short years later I went out into the garden one day and that little tree was fourteen feet tall but still in no way maturing. At that point I knew for sure it wasn't a pear tree, but I didn't know what it was. I was curious, but busy, and not curious enough to stop what I was doing and find out, which is ridiculous, since it would have only taken about five minutes for me to snap a shot of the leaves and the bark and send it to one of my nurserymen. But sometimes we think our schedules are way more important than they really are. Usually, in fact.

Though I always seemed to think I didn't have time to ID this tree, I was never too busy to go outside and watch a storm blow in. It's one of the things I will miss the most when I move out to California.

The skies darkened as I settled myself outside to relish this incoming storm. Clouds were rolling in fast. There was thunder in the distance. A flash of lightning. I could see a strong gust of wind coming toward me from the east as treetops suddenly began to dance and sway with greater and greater animation. As the wind hit the giant cottonwood down the street, I could hear its clattering leaves like tiny castanets creating the building beat of the storm. And then it happened. Just behind me, to the west in the garden, I heard an echo. Loud rustling like a response to the call of the giant cottonwood almost four hundred feet away. Call and response…call and response. It was a cottonwood! The little unidentified, oversized duckling in my garden was really a swan! A cottonwood that had found its voice. I had been looking at that little tree for two years, trying to figure out who it was, and all I really needed to do was close my eyes and listen to it. I can honestly say it was the first time in my life I had ever identified a plant by *listening* to it. But there it was. This gangly adolescent that was tall but not yet wide had reached a height where it could catch the wind, and with that first deep breath, its song poured forth in a voice that was ready to be heard.

My voice, too, is ready to be heard. When my marriage fell apart, I knew from the beginning that the biggest reason—maybe the only reason—was our failure to communicate effectively. Or at all, toward the end. I figured out far too late that Daniel was intimacy avoidant, and I was so desperate to connect that I was terrified to do anything that might make him withdraw or reject me further. How ironic. The exact thing I was trying to avoid was what I facilitated by never saying what I wanted and needed to say. By trying not to rock the boat, I inadvertently capsized it altogether. I take responsibility for that, but to be fair, Daniel didn't invite intimacy often. Not the kind of intimacy I longed for. The kind that involves deep, soul-baring conversations. Indeed, I don't think we ever had a single conversation like that in over thirty years.

But once—just once, he said to me, "I cannot know what

you're thinking unless you tell me." He was right. I knew he was. But by the time he said it, ten years into our marriage, it was too late. It didn't feel safe. I can't really blame him for that, although he is partly to blame.

But my fear of speaking out was born, nurtured, and developed years before he and I ever met. I had been hushed my whole life. Hushed, scolded, and made to fear the consequences of sharing my fragile thoughts and deepest fears. It didn't feel safe because it wasn't. And he didn't feel safe because he wasn't either. Not in that way. Daniel's vulnerability avoidance was practiced, and his boundaries around it were solid. So I shook my head and said, "I'm fine," which was probably the most damaging lie I've ever told in my life, and I told it over and over and over again.

Listening to this enthusiastic little soloist in my garden, singing along with the matriarch down the street while also catching its own breezes, shimmering with a chorus all its own, moved something deep within me. This was the little girl who always raised her hand in class, before that became uncool. This was the adolescent girl who loved being front and center at the volleyball net so she could spike the ball fast and hard, before that became unfeminine. This was the college girl who dreamed of being a translator for the United Nations, before she began to believe she wasn't smart enough for that or, if she was, no boy would ever want her. This was the girl who was pure promise. Anxious to be heard. Oblivious to the doubts of others. Joyous, unfettered, unsilenced.

I thought I had been paying attention to that little tree.

I had wondered about its identity. I had watched it for clues. But the information hadn't yielded easy answers, so I moved on. What I needed to do was be still, tune in, and listen. How often in relationships is that all we really need to give or to receive? Just listen. Listen, without expectation, without judgment, and without defense.

If you want to know me, then please...just listen.

A New Day

I have lived in Texas for a lot of years, but it still surprises me how searingly hot it can be in the summer, even at night, and I don't like it. Although I consider myself to be a glass-is-half-full kind of girl, I admit, on probably countless occasions, I have been known to whine about the heat here. In fact, when it's hot outside—really hot—it would probably be fair to say I can be a real complainer.

On this morning, I had been awakened very early by a loud sound. It was around five o'clock. I couldn't identify the sound, but from my sleepy, groggy consciousness, I thought it might have been the emergency weather siren, so I got up to see. As I looked out through my bedroom's glass doors, the colors of the garden were barely discernible in the dark, gray night light. I walked outside, braced for the heat, but before I had a chance to do my usual eye roll and sigh, and run my regularly scheduled program of "how in the world can it be this hot this early in the morning?" my senses were struck full on with the strong, saturating scent of jasmine, which was so thick and heavy in the moist, hot air I almost lost my balance. The sensation was unique and completely disorienting because it was more than olfactory. I could actually feel the fragrance. It felt like a sweet shawl wrapping around me. It had weight. It had substance. It had density. It was as if the air that held the fragrance was so heavy with its floral fare, it was leaning on me to share the weight. The experience was so powerful and so beautiful, I felt emotion move through me in a different way than I had ever felt before.

Somewhat more awake now, and held in this gentle but powerful sensation, I steadied myself, walked farther into the garden, and looked up. No storm. Not even any clouds. But instead of the usual disappointment, accompanied by the old "of course not, it's summer in Texas" refrain, as I scanned the sky, I caught my breath. Venus was huge! Jupiter, too. And there was Orion, brighter and clearer than I had ever seen it. I stood motionless, held now by both the sweetness of the scented air and the sparkling beauty in the sky. Immersed in the thick, heady fragrant air, I felt I was a part of the air and by extension, the sky. Terrestrial and celestial, one with the earth and the sky. And as I stood in the moonlight, senses awash in this concert of jasmine and starlight, for the first time in my life I was filled with a deep appreciation for the heat of the summer night and the fact that I could stand outside in this beautiful phenomenon for as long as I wanted without shivering, or breaking the spell by needing to go in from the chill. I could stay in that warm, sweet morning moment and experience myself not just in my garden, but as my garden. Not in the universe, but as the Universe. A lucid oneness unlike any I had ever touched, even in meditation. Grace and gratitude surged through me as this new perspective opened my heart to the joy of being able to stand there in my flimsy nightgown and feel the fragrance of the jasmine on my skin without the need for a sweater or my old story about summer nights in Texas. To have a completely different impression of the warm, close summer morning, and the expansive, infinite world. I could experience not just another day, but a new day. And because of it, I, too, was new.

Raucous Raccoons

I like living in harmony with nature. I try to be at peace with caterpillars eating my herbs and flowers because I love to see them transform into butterflies and moths in my garden. I have no problem with wasps building nests around my house because they keep the aforementioned caterpillars and other pesky insects from overrunning the garden so I don't have to use any kind of control treatments—not even organic ones. I wouldn't want a spider as a pet, but I adore the beauty of their webs, and I honor and appreciate the work they do in the garden as well. I love my beautiful lizards and anoles, and even respect the work of snakes in the web of life in my garden.

Stepping up the food chain, I have made my peace with bunnies who are so cute, but always cost me a small fortune as I constantly need to replant the seasonal flowers they devour. And I gave up long ago on ever eating any vegetables I grew because the squirrels always got to them first. It's annoying, but I can live with that. I'm not trying to feed myself from my garden, and they are hilarious running across the yard and up the trees trying to maneuver around a zucchini that is twice their size. It's worth the loss in produce to have the comedy outside.

I also share my territory with foxes, bobcats, and coyotes, for whom I have enough respect that I rarely walk into the depths of my garden when I am outside after sunset, and I make my presence audibly known in response to rustling in the garden's wild, dark corners, lest they become startled and we both regret it. All these creatures and I have an understanding. I respect and avoid them; they respect and avoid me. They eat my stuff, but that's okay.

Then there are the raccoons.

Depending on my mood, it usually amuses me and sometimes annoys me that the raccoons think they have an all season pass to everything in my garden, including my swimming pool. Several times a year, usually in the spring and summer, they wake me up with their animated chittering, and I look outside to see three or four young ones tussling, rolling around, and chasing each other, tearing through my flower beds with boisterous abandon, oblivious and fully indifferent to the care with which I tend those beds. They are so comfortable in my garden that on one recent spring night, I had the doors open in my bedroom, and two juveniles about the size of my cats walked right over to the door, pressing their little noses against the screen, curious about what I was doing. My cats came over in stealth mode and stopped about a foot away from the screen, crouched behind the ottoman. They were not at all sure about these strange, masked interlopers. Then, in a flash from stage left, a third raccoon came running around the corner at full tilt, slamming into the other two. And like a scene from the Keystone Cops, a fourth careened into the first three, and the whole crowd turned into a Looney Tunes tumble of rolling, yipping, scrambling paws and tails.

The raccoons regularly dig up my garden looking for worms and grubs. Apparently there was a significant supply of deliciousness in my peony bed one year, and they trashed three of my favorite peonies digging around them. They pulled over a beautiful Celtic birdbath, which cracked in two when it hit the patio. They have even figured out that there are tender morsels up in flowerpots they have to scale to reach, which they seem to find worth the effort. And this past summer, on several different occasions, I have been awakened to loud exchanges of wild hilarity as three or four or even five of these little banditos ran around my pool yelling at others who were in the pool swimming around, having water fights and playing Who's King of the Mountain with my foam raft. Honestly, if they weren't so adorable, they would be *super* annoying!

One recent night, I had been on the phone late and was very tired, but I had heated the spa earlier and wanted to go out to enjoy it before I went to bed. As I sat in the hot, soothing water, I laid my head back, resting it against the side of the spa, and closed my eyes. I relaxed there for ten minutes or so. When I opened my eyes, I was a bit startled to see a raccoon approaching along the left side of the pool beside the steps. She was not a juvenile, but not full grown either.

"Oh!" I exclaimed, which would normally be enough to make a wild creature retreat.

"Well, hello there," I said when she didn't react to my presence.

"So...what's up, dude?" I asked as I slowly stood up in the spa, remaining in place while also making myself bigger.

By this time, she had stopped about five feet away from me, holding my gaze. I might have discerned a scowl.

"I know it's later than I am usually out here," I explained. "Were you planning on using the spa tonight?"

She didn't answer. She just leaned down and took a drink out of the pool.

When she looked back up, I said, "Aren't you supposed to be scared of me or something?"

With that, she took a few more steps toward me, then dipped down onto the first step of the pool into the water and sat down, slightly angled away from me, and began to wash her paws and face.

"I guess not..."

At this point she was so close, I could have reached over and touched her.

"Pardon me if I'm interfering with your evening ablutions," I said, "but since I pay the water bill, it seems only fair that I should get first dibs."

She basically ignored me while she got her little nose, paws, and muzzle all shiny and clean; then she lay down in the water that covered the top step for a few minutes. I was puzzled but had no serious objections, being aware that although we don't have an agreement in writing, it was clear I was the one who had overstepped our accepted time-share allocation of the resort facilities.

"All righty," I said. "Well, you just let me know if you need anything else, missy." And I sat back down to watch her.

Ten minutes or so later, she climbed out of the pool and moseyed on around the edge of the water, taking the long way back through the rosemary and the flowering evergreen oregano. Wide awake now, I went inside and did a little research to see if there was something I might have been missing with all this raccoon activity in my immediate proximity. What I read made me literally laugh out loud.

Some native cultures say that when raccoons come into your life, it is time to let go. You are being invited to release something. It could be a person, or a belief system, or a fear; it could be a job, a way of life, a habit, or really anything that you are clinging to that might no longer serve you. And since I have more than my fair share of things to let go of, and a disproportionately high number of raccoons in my garden (at least three litters a season), I'm thinking maybe I should pay attention. Of course, I already knew I had trouble letting go. It's one of the main themes about which I muse. But perhaps what this little lady was saying when she sat down was, "This is no longer a suggestion. You've waited long enough. It's time for you to let go! I'll just wait right here while you figure that out."

Bossy.

Apparently raccoons also invite you to go within and ask yourself what is stopping you, if you are willing to accept the gifts the Universe is offering you, and why you do not trust.

Why is it always my fault?!

Oh…right…because it's *my* life, and I get to choose whether to live it boldly and passionately, with courage and authenticity, or go silently into the night, carefully guarding my quiet desperation.

Man, those straight-talkin' raccoons don't fool around. I feel pretty exposed right now. Kind of like that time I was staying with my friend Mary at her place in Ojai and I was reciting my same old refrain about all the things I felt I couldn't do until I lost weight. She listened to that for about as long as I guess she could stand it, and then she said, "I just want to know when you're going to start living your life."

Ouch.

Well, you know what they say: The Universe will whisper to you. Then it will call to you. Then it will shout to you. Then it sends in the raccoons.

A Prairie Dog
Companion

It is both fascinating and mortifying to think about how many things I have not done in my life because of how I felt about my body. I didn't come by these feelings in a vacuum, of course. That's not how self-hatred works. Indeed, I didn't come by them at all. They were given to me. A gift of meanness and malice that keeps on giving decades later. I don't remember how far back it began, but I do remember where, and who started it.

Bon Bon had a classic flapper figure. Tallish and straight up and down. No bust, no waist, no hips, no behind, she naturally possessed the perfect boyish form for the iconic loose, dropped-waist, tubular dresses of the Roaring Twenties. Dresses made of beautiful, often heavily embellished fabrics sewn in diaphanous, shapeless silhouettes. She didn't have to flatten her breasts, as many women did, to wear the fashions of the day. She had the ideal body for her era.

With strength born of a rugged childhood growing up on a farm in Illinois in the late 1800s, a passionate determination to live a more worldly life, and more courage than I can fathom, Bon Bon (Bonnie) joined the American Red Cross (prior to the founding of the USO) when World War I broke out, and went to sing for the Allied troops in Europe. Bon Bon remained daring, rail thin, and very chic her whole life.

Grandma, my maternal grandmother, was the opposite of Bon Bon in almost every way. Born Sarah Elizabeth (Besse), she had a voluptuous figure and held to the more traditional Gibson Girl style in her youth, fashions that emphasized her fuller bust and hips, with a small waist. Descended from German immigrants who were among the first six families to settle in what is now Tarrant County, Texas (which includes Fort Worth), Besse was one of four daughters whose only little brother had died in infancy and whose father had died at twenty-eight. She was much more of a homebody. Indeed, Grandma never even learned how to drive. She had been considered a great beauty in her youth and still had an enviable complexion when she died at ninety-two. She was a wonderful cook, and as she got older, she became very overweight.

Mama had a combination of Grandma's shapely figure and Bon Bon's eye for sophistication and fashion. It was obvious what my father saw in her. That, and the fact that everyone loved her. I am shaped like my maternal side.

Bon Bon despised both Mama and Grandma. She hated Mama for "taking away" her only son. I don't know why she hated Grandma, but I expect it had something to do with how Grandma's speech was peppered with country colloquialisms, which reminded Bon Bon of the rural upbringing she had done everything she could to leave behind. But of all the things Bon Bon despised about Grandma, the thing she felt she had permission to be most vocal about was her weight.

I, on the other hand, adored Grandma. She was cushy and comforting, loving and funny, kind and down-to-earth. And her macaroni and cheese, and refrigerator milk chocolate cupcakes, were out of this world. Bon Bon lived in a big house in Highland Park. She was rich and glamorous, but she was also angry, bitter, and cruel. She had returned to the States after the war, where she met and married a wealthy Texan, and moved with him to his small hometown in northeast Texas. But "how ya gonna keep 'em down on the farm after they've seen Paree?" As "a Yankee," Bonnie never felt accepted by the local girls, and was miserable being back in Small Town, USA, particularly in the South. So she divorced my grandfather when my father was a toddler (both brave and scandalous in 1929), and moved to the nearest city—Dallas.

The story of why my mother didn't protect me from Bon Bon's cruelty is one of misguided good intentions, but suffice it to say, Bon Bon's brutal verbal abuse was the beginning of a lifelong struggle against my weight and myself. I adopted a state of self-loathing because I was told I was loathsome, over and over, at every opportunity, from the moment my mother announced she was pregnant with me until the day Bon Bon died when I was in my midtwenties.

As I have learned in my years of therapy, it's not surprising that I would bring other people into my life who would also be cruel and critical about my weight, among other things. I don't understand how that works, but here's what I do know: Even when I was a fashion model and almost dangerously thin, stumpy, trollish fashion photographers would critique my body, shaming me for having curves as a power move to disarm me while trying to seduce me. Of course, I didn't put that modus operandi together at the time. I just starved myself, hated myself, and hated my body.

On some of the many occasions when I have traveled to Taos, New Mexico, I have stayed at an historic inn with large rooms on the back which face a vast, open field. This field is home to dozens, maybe hundreds of prairie dogs that dash around day in and day out foraging for food. Every few minutes, one or more will suddenly sit up on their hind legs and freeze, startled by a sound or movement that might signal problems. After a few sniffs of the air and a quick scan of the territory, they will *yip, yip, yip*, and everyone will either freeze or dash into their mounds, depending on the *yip*. This ritual goes on dozens of times a day and is endlessly amusing to me. I adore these little chubbettes and their hypervigilance.

On a recent sojourn in Taos, I asked for one of those rear-facing rooms, and was charmed each day to observe how precisely the prairie dogs emerged from their mounds as the sun came across the field. They did not all emerge when the sun began to rise—they emerged when the sunlight moved across the field, awakening each mound. And as the sun began to set, with a less defined line than when it rose, they filtered home one by one, mothers herding their little ones, tucking into their burrows for the night.

As I watched these darling furry fuzz balls, I observed how strong, quick, and agile they are, and yet, they are quite fat little friends, with very plush tummies and rear ends. I found myself feeling a poignant pang of longing. What would it be like to be so unselfconscious of one's body? How lovely would it be to embrace one's form with absolute acceptance? I honestly cannot even imagine it.

As for me, I am never enough. Or more accurately, I am always too much. Or even more accurately, I'm always too much, and therefore never enough. Or so I've always been told.

I recently had an opportunity to meet with a life coach who had written several books that had sold moderately well. His focus was on helping businesspeople figure out how they limit themselves or sabotage their own success and how to stop that. He was an elderly man who had long since stopped seeing clients, but we had a friend in common, so one day when I was going to be traveling to visit her, she offered to see if he would meet with me. I honestly didn't really feel the need. I didn't see that I had any active self-sabotaging issues at the time, but as she and I talked, my feelings about all the things I stop myself from doing because of my weight came up. Long story short, she convinced me I should meet with him. He tentatively agreed but wanted to do a video vetting before committing, which I confess kind of triggered me. I told her, "I am not even the one who wants to see this guy, and now I have to audition? Give me a break." But she convinced me it would be worth it given how my life was unfolding at the time, so I agreed.

In the video call he asked how I was holding myself back. I told him what was going on in my life and all the ways in which I postponed or deflected opportunities because of worries about my weight, regardless of whether I was overweight, normal weight, or even underweight, all of which I have been . . . repeatedly. "We can work with that," he said, and we booked an appointment for when I was going to be in town.

I met with him at his home office. A small, slight, frail-looking man, he asked me to remind him what the circumstances of my life were at the time and how I felt I was sabotaging myself. I told him again about my recent exciting opportunities and how fearful I felt about stepping into some of the more public aspects at my current weight, to which he replied, "Yeah, I think you need to do something drastic like bariatric surgery."

Wait . . . what?

He went on, "When I was going to be on TV, I even sprang for $18,000 to cap my teeth." He flashed a lipless smile. "You don't want to look like a country rube. And if you don't look the part, they won't ask you back."

In hindsight, I wish I had taken the opportunity to break

it to the old guy that he was never on TV because of his looks, but hindsight of this nature is always 20/20 and I'm never really that mean in person—more from cowardice than kindness. But for once, I'm pretty sure I wasn't the one suffering from body dysmorphia.

He went on to ask me how much I wanted to weigh. This was *so not* what I came for, but every disempowered drop of blood in my body was ignited, and I found myself emotionally collapsing, and just going along, instead of blasting him, which is what I should have done. When I answered with a "goal weight," he raised his eyebrows skeptically and paused. He finally wrote the number down, but he clearly didn't think it was low enough. So, a few minutes later, he circled back around pretending to be subtle, and mentioned his own weight, which was only ten pounds more than my "goal" weight. But he was a shriveled little grandpappy! What possible relevance could his weight have in this context?

And by the way, does this guy have *any idea* how off brand he is right now?

I was honestly so floored, and so triggered, I think I completely dissociated. I robotically went through the motions of the rest of the session, but I was in no way present. I remember answering his questions. I remember him pointing out all the books he had written on his bookshelves—twice. At one point, in an almost comical display of projection, he told me he was from a small town and had never had a fresh vegetable until he was in his late twenties. Then he began to explain to me the most basic fundamentals of dieting, as if I couldn't recite the dos, don'ts, and details of virtually every diet book that had been written since 1975. But all I could think about was that he was supposed to be giving me tools to rise above my fears about my weight, and instead, he was not only confirming my fears, but was aggressively amplifying every one of them. And I do feel compelled to say—not that it should make any difference at all, but for reference— it's not like I needed to be removed from my house by a crane. I mean, I was heavier than I had ever been before, but I was still shopping in regular stores, for heaven's sake. But this shallow, one-dimensional, misogynistic old man, with zero clue about my history or what might have happened to me, my body, or my spirit to influence my weight, made a thousand assumptions about me that had literally no basis in reality—all of them rooted in his personal opinion about my looks. He had reduced me to nothing more than a dress size, when I had just landed an amazing opportunity that could change not only my career but my life, *because of my work*. I should have screamed at this man, *"I AM MORE THAN MY LOOKS. YOU ARE SUPPOSED TO BE HELPING ME GROUND IN THAT TRUTH!"*

But instead, I said nothing. It frankly never crossed my mind to stop him as it was happening. I was so used to this particular brand of abuse, my mind just separated from my body. I sat there, compliant. Frozen in a protracted flashback of every experience of abuse of power and male diminishment from my past where I had been reduced to a mere physical form that had value or not depending on the degree to which a man found me pleasing. I sat there and nodded as if he was saying something—anything—that might have had even a teeny tiny drop of value, which he definitely was not. Just like Bon Bon and Daniel and countless fashion photographers and my college boyfriend and every other person who had discounted or completely dismissed everything else about me except my physical appearance, this so-called expert on breaking your own glass ceiling had reflexively thrown me against a ceiling of titanium because he thought I needed to lose weight. He basically told me I had already failed in this dream career opportunity if I didn't submit to surgical violence against my body and wrestle it into his opinion of television-appropriate submission.

As I was leaving, he told me he would like me to stay in touch with him. That he would like to continue our "coaching" once a month. And you know what I did? I thanked him. Not only that, I actually put it on my digital calendar to email him in a month, with a repeat alert for every month going forward.

When I got into my car, the only thing I remember thinking was, "I wish I had my $500 back," as I drove to my hotel.

When I got there, I called my friend Sophia, who was taking care of my house and my cats while I was gone. I might have been numb from the experience, but Sophia definitely was not. As I was too deeply immersed in my archaic wounds to really react myself, Sophia stepped up on my behalf, and basically Hulked out on the phone, furiously and indignantly defending me and pointing out, among many other things, that he never in a million years would have said any of that to me if I had been a man.

Yep.

And I know I am not the only one who suffers from this unfairness. I know that one of the main causes of excessive weight gain and retention, particularly among women, is past abuse, neglect, or trauma. It's frequently sexual abuse, but it can be any kind. So why do people feel they have permission to further traumatize these abuse survivors just because the evidence of their suffering makes them heavy? Anybody who knows anything about abuse survivors *knows* this is often a symptom. Why don't diets work? Because with so many people who are overweight, *it is not about food.* But there are billions of dollars to be made by making people believe their weight is a mere product of not eating right and not exercising enough. And if they can wrap it up in a shiny package and say, "We're just concerned about your health," then they can be as relentlessly brutal as they want, because they're "just trying to help." The reality is when people criticize you because of your weight, no matter what they say, it's rarely about health. It's about aesthetics.

But what if every woman who is overweight because of past abuse were covered in bloody bruises and scars instead of fat? Would society treat them differently?

The smart money says, "You bet it would."

My dream is that every time we see someone who is very overweight, instead of dismissing them as lazy, overindulgent gluttons who offend our sensibilities and clearly lack discipline, we consider that perhaps we are looking at someone whose body is desperately trying to protect them and keep them safe from suffering we cannot imagine. How different would the world be if we were willing to see weight through the eyes of compassion instead of judgment? Maybe 70 percent of Americans aren't overweight or obese because of gluten or carbs or lectins or GMOs or a lack of sufficient exercise. Maybe it's because we're so mean to each other.

A few weeks later, as I sat on the balcony in Taos watching all those beautiful, chubby little prairie dogs, so affectionately grooming and nuzzling each other, clearly loving each other exactly as they were, I took their message into meditation, as the prairie dog invites us to do. Prairie dog's message is an invitation to retreat into ourselves. They invite us to observe them, and take our own metaphorical deep dive into the underworld of our souls, to dig down into our psyches and reemerge from the darkness of this heroic journey with a replenished spirit and a new, more enlightened perspective.

As I dived into my deeper consciousness, this is what I found. The truth is, I am the common denominator. It is I who deeply disapproves of my body. It is I who constantly maligns and berates it. It is I who frequently starves myself hoping maybe this is the diet that will finally melt the shame from my thighs. It is I who believes no one could ever accept me as I am. I didn't light the fire, but I have kept it burning all these years by believing it to be true. These days, it all originates right here.

An interesting thing happened after my meeting with

the hypocritical life coach from hell. After I left, I felt something...a new sensation I could not identify at first. But soon, as I dialed into it, I understood it was a deep sense of how wrong he was. I felt it in my core. For once in my life, I didn't believe a man when he told me I wasn't enough because of my body. For the first time, I truly, deeply did not believe that I was finished before I started with this wonderful opportunity if I didn't have surgeons of questionable motivation carve away parts of the only body that has ever stuck with me and tried to support and protect me no matter what happened.

This body...this beautiful, resilient, responsive, supportive body is the *only* thing that has never betrayed me. It has always and only ever tried to protect me in the one way it knew how. And in that moment, a shift happened. I felt grateful for my body. Deeply grateful. Grateful for every pound. Because each and every pound is a measure of the degree to which I have felt lost, abandoned, wounded, alone, unloved, and afraid. Like notches on a gun barrel in the Old West, every pound is a record, not of my failure as a human but of my experience as one. My body is the most consistent, accurate measure of the state of my mind and my heart, and it always, always, always tells the truth. When I am too triggered or too deep in my wounds to know how I truly feel, I can always trust my body to tell me. Why would I ever cut apart the only eternally trustworthy truth speaker in my life?

One month to the day after our meeting, when the first notification popped up on my digital calendar to contact the world's worst life coach, I felt a sick feeling in my stomach. I delayed the message, and it popped up again several times over the next few days. I reasoned that he had contacts, he had experience, it was possible he could be helpful. Maybe I shouldn't burn this bridge. But I could never bring myself to so much as open a draft for an email to him. Three months later, after I had delayed and ultimately dismissed each notification to reconnect with him, when it popped up again, I took a deep breath in and asked myself, "Is this someone with whom you would like to share the wonder and joy that is flowing into your life?" The answer returned as a resounding *no*.

With that I deleted the notification, and when I did, a window dropped down that gave me an option: "You are deleting a recurring event. Do you want to delete this and all future occurrences of this event, or only the selected occurrence?"

I clicked "Delete All Future Events." Yes, I want to delete from my life all future occurrences of this event. And the people who would create them.

Today, I have made a change. I now make a point to notice the ways in which my body reacts to protect me. Now, instead of making it wrong, I thank it, and I ask how I can be of better support, so it feels safe and does not feel the need to build walls around me to protect and support me. I also make a point to periodically thank my body simply for functioning as it should—for waking up in the morning, for digesting food as designed, for holding me steadily in place in a yoga posture. I am finally aware of all the amazing ways in which my body serves me so perfectly, and I am deeply grateful. Better late than never. Sure, I would rather not have had to endure the shallow, insensitive judgment of that dreadful little man, but here was the gift: I realized my worries about self-sabotage regarding my weight no longer really exist. I assumed they did, because that is the oldest story in my playbook. But when it got right down to it, I didn't need advice, guidance, ideas, or a tool from him or anyone else for how to get my belief systems under control. All I needed to do was show my body the same love and compassion I show to others. It took this one last attack to finally make me see that I was not at war with my body at all. I never was. The baton of cruel assaults on my body had been passed to me, first by Bon Bon, then by anyone and everyone else from whom I would accept it. Which, for most of my life, was anyone and everyone. But I can tell you this: That was the last time. Never again will I allow myself to be so rudely spoken to, nor allow judgment about my body by a lesser-evolved mortal to be spoken in my presence. I am releasing that baton like a mic drop.

Peace out.

Chop Wood, Carry Water

I can always find solace in the garden. Solace, and often answers. I don't ever go into the garden looking for answers, but that is where they often find me. There is no one particular kind of garden that most soothes my spirit, though I do love the ones with lots of flowers. But I will take what I can get as long as it's green, as I know they all hold wisdom.

On this day, I had sought refuge in a small courtyard garden at a church near my home. It was a lovely Gothic church that reminded me of my childhood in Europe. Outside the sanctuary there was a small, sweet garden where I always knew I could sit in quiet solitude, having never shared the space with another soul in all the years I had visited. The garden is slightly sunken, and formal in design with a very simple planting of holly trees all the way around to create a green enclosure. I remember thinking when the planting went in that it was a mistake. The concept was good, but I knew the holly trees they had chosen were eventually going to get too big for the space, which would become a problem down the road.

Sure enough, when I went this time, my worst fears had been realized. The hollies had indeed grown too large for their placement, and some clueless maintenance crew had just tried to butcher them into conformity. Now, instead of four lovely, lush, green walls, I was surrounded by a bony, grotesque monument to poor planning, bad execution, and worse maintenance. I thought (with no small amount of smugness) about how much better I could have done it. I thought about how I would have selected more appropriate plants in the first place. How I would have designed the beds to be bigger and more accommodating. How I would have cared for the trees so much more attentively, treated them so much more kindly, pruned them so much more carefully. How I would have loved them into thriving health.

I closed my eyes, both to block out the horticultural vandalism this garden had suffered and to go within, which was why I came here in the first place. Trying to center in the stillness, annoyance remained in my mind and my body. I could not seem to let go of how badly this garden had been treated. Angry, irritated thoughts permeated my mind, with an ongoing side chorus of how much better I could have done it. I didn't want to sit in this irritation. It was disproportionate to the impact this courtyard should have on my life. I have learned, over these years of spiritual and psychological study, that a process of inquiry can be most edifying when something or someone bothers me. Especially when they bother me a lot for no obvious reason. So I dialed into the feelings and asked myself:

"Why does this irritate you so much?"

"Isn't it obvious? They are not taking care of these beautiful trees at all. Are they blind to how they're ruining them? Can't they see how they're hurting them? Can't they see how terrible they look now?"

"Where in your life have you done the same thing?"

"Excuse me?! I would never do this in a million years!"

"Yes, but where in your life have you done it?"

"Nowhere!"

"Is it possible you might have? Somewhere?"

" . . . ?"

I wanted to continue to defend, but I couldn't. The question mattered. I could feel it. So I sat in the discomfort until the urge to defend began to fade, at which point I actually heard the question. Not the question I thought was being asked, but the real question. And in the presence of the real question, a real answer rose up and began to take form within me.

Yes, I knew how to care for plants. I knew how to care for trees. I knew how to care for people. I was a doting "pet mom." I knew how to care for every other living thing on this earth. But I still had no idea how to care for myself. Not really. Not in an ongoing, nonreactive, genuinely loving way. I gave and gave and gave love, hoping against hope that if I gave enough, it would somehow translate into being loved in return. But I had it wrong. I had always done it all wrong.

I had loved Dan so much, I thought sacrificing my own feelings and absorbing his anger would somehow make things better. But that was the worst thing I could have done. It caused me immeasurable pain, lasting wounds, and ultimately led to the end of our marriage.

I had loved Glenn so much that when I discovered he was more than friends with someone else, I jumped through countless hoops and suffered for years trying to allow him to have it both ways. Even after the big blowup, I tried for a few months to restore what we had lost, in large part, to keep him from feeling the full brunt of his actions and my pain.

I had always loved not wisely, but too well.

Since childhood, I had not known how to ask for what I wanted. And it is also true that I was terrible at receiving. When people gave me nice things, I felt guilty. Every time. I never, ever felt truly worthy of gifts that had been given to me—not from people, or from the Universe. I was in my forties before I ever got a *manicure*. And it was not (as I had always claimed) just because I had bitten my fingernails ever since my father died. It was because it felt so indulgent. I didn't like being touched in such an intimate way. Especially not by a stranger. It seemed creepy to me. Same with massages. I was mortified the first time someone gave me a massage as a gift. The idea of that level of vulnerability, that kind of touch, felt super uncomfortable. I let that gift certificate expire. I wouldn't even wear rubber gloves when I washed the dishes (even though my mother constantly admonished me to do so) because it felt too self-pampering. I was just now realizing, I was the most withholding person in my life. I was the one who would never give myself the small, simple kindnesses I so freely offered to every other living thing with whom I came into contact. I didn't think I deserved the same, so I not only accepted less, I insisted on it, actively refusing the loving gestures of others.

Sitting amongst these woody, mutilated, skeletal holly trees, this tragic insinuation of beauty that might have been, I suddenly realized why I hated *The Giving Tree. I was the giving tree!* The book was simply a mirror whose reflection I could not bear. I was the one who had given and given until I had almost nothing left to give and then invited everyone to sit on me. The hand that cut me was my own, both figuratively and sometimes, literally.

When this hit me, it hit me hard. A cascade of realizations like a Hevesh5 domino design, where a lifetime of wounds, fears, beliefs, assumptions, and self-destructive, protective habits collapsed, one after another, into a spectacular clattering heap. I suddenly, finally, got it. I was the missing piece I had been looking for. I was the one who constantly criticized me. I was the one who couldn't accept my body. I was the one who didn't think I was smart enough. I was the one who didn't think I was pretty enough. I was the one who found fault in everything I did and called it perfectionism because that made it more palatable. I was the one who stopped me from reaching for my dreams. I was the one who punished me. I was the one who was constantly with-holding anything and everything that might feel nurturing. I was the one who never, ever thought I was enough. I was the one who...didn't love me.

I had always rejected the concept of self-love. To me, it was synonymous with self-indulgence, and that was not something I was willing to engage in. I had ignored Barbara when she gave me exercises to be kinder to myself. Even as I opened myself to the concepts of self-care, I continued to reject self-love. I had trouble saying the words without a sarcastic tone. I have trouble writing them now. I had grasped pieces of this puzzle. I had had moments of insight in this vein. But I had never fully put it together. Even when I had several pieces that fit with each other, making a large segment of the puzzle clear, I never before truly un-derstood the far greater issue. I never saw the picture I was trying to create. Until today.

The path to self-awareness and understanding is a twisty, uphill road with a lot of switchbacks. There are no guardrails on some of the steepest, narrowest, most treach-erous curves. The unlit tunnels are many, and they're all extremely long. The road to self-awareness reminds me of a sign at a wilderness trailhead I once heard about that read YOU ARE NOW ENTERING THE FOOD CHAIN. This is raw re-ality. It is harsh, unvarnished truth. This isn't some dandy hike through nature where you summit tired and a little sweaty. This is the Hunger Games.

And FYI, don't believe them when they say "awareness" gets you 90 percent of the way there. I've had a boatload of awareness for a decade or more. Awareness is not understanding. It's key, but it is just the first teeny tiny step in the slow unfurling of a life so rich and messy and full of experience, so tightly woven into such a beautiful, complicated, detailed tapestry, you will hardly believe it is yours.

You want to know what makes you tick? You want to find the source of your wounding and heal it? Well, I applaud you. Just know this: It's not for the lily-livered. It is a lot of responsibility to realize there is no one else to blame. In fact, it's all the responsibility. It is shattering to discover you were your problem all along, and I have a feeling it's not just me who discovers this is the realization to be found at the end of the proverbial rainbow. Self-discovery is a one step forward, two steps back—right off the edge of a cliff process. Then you crawl your way back up on your hands and knees and begin again. And again. And again.

There is a Zen saying: "Before enlightenment, chop wood, carry water. After enlightenment, chop wood, carry water." In other words, enlightenment isn't your own personal Rapture. Enlightenment is transcendent understanding of the human experience. Deep, cellular understanding. It is realization at its most profound, and acceptance of the truth you have discovered. It is taking responsibility for this knowledge and everything else in your life going forward.

And then, your life goes on. Chop wood, carry water. But this time, you do it unburdened from the pain of your past and the fear for your future. Awakening changes everything. How you understand the past, how you live in the present, and how you move into the future. As the scales fall from your eyes, the world shimmers with love, compassion, and forgiveness. You chop wood and carry water with a new awareness that everything you touch, say, and do is a sacrament.

Your life does not change. What changes is how you experience it.

The Sanskrit word *bodhi*, which is often translated as "enlightenment," can also be translated as "awakening." I'm more comfortable with this definition because enlightenment feels like completion, an end point, while awakening feels more like a step in the process. A big step, but just a step. And I know I am only standing on a step in my process. Most of my unconscious is still unconscious, and ever will be. But I have awakened to some profound truths that do not just apply to me. I believe this is the point at which personal work becomes an awakening, where we can see how our suffering connects us, and thus is elevated to a more universal plain. Where we can see how our struggles are not unique, nor are they even just our own. I believe awakening is the point in our journey when we discover we are one.

Brother ChiSing, founder of the Dallas Meditation Center, used to call sangha members bodhisattvas—those who choose to help ease the suffering of others and are moving in the direction of Buddha (which simply means "awakened one"). It felt like a loving oversell at the time. Like a dad calling his daughter a princess. But maybe I'm not giving myself enough credit. It wouldn't be the first time. Maybe what Brother ChiSing was saying was we are all bodhisattvas because life is hard and it takes courage to get up every day and face it. Maybe he was saying that if we can even glimpse our interconnectedness, we have achieved uncommon wisdom. Maybe we are bodhisattvas simply because we are trying.

When I opened my eyes and looked around me, the little church courtyard had changed. Instead of being encircled with hideously mistreated holly trees, I was surrounded by giving trees whose sacrifice had guided me to a profound new understanding of myself. I smiled as I remembered (because I was born at Christmas) that my mother had almost named me Holly. When I looked at these arboreal sisters now, I saw the beauty of their wounds, the depth of their gifts. I felt their resilience.

We teach people how to treat us. I'm ready for a new lesson plan.

Blank Canvas

When I first bought this house, one of the things I loved about it was that the whole package—the house and the surrounding lot—was essentially a blank canvas. The house was a mess inside and out, and the "garden" in front consisted of a row of woody, butchered hollies on the east side, a row of chlorotic liriope in an otherwise empty flower bed on the west side, one large white oleander at the corner, and a Bradford pear tree by the street. In back there were two pink crape myrtle trees that were too close to the house and each other, three leggy white crape myrtles along the back fence that never bloomed, two mulberry trees, two hackberry trees, and the glorious, ancient trumpet vine that ran for twenty feet along the west side and arched gracefully toward the patio off my bedroom.

Over the fourteen years that I have been in this house, much has changed. I was married to Dan when I moved in. We separated within fifteen months. During the eight years of our separation, seven of those years were spent in a crisis of fear and self-doubt. The last year saw me commit to my own salvation, as I stepped up and built a thriving, prosperous business. Six of those years I spent loving Glenn. I have now been divorced from Dan for four years, most of them also without Glenn.

Over the same fourteen years, the hollies in front were moved and transplanted and are now eight-foot-tall mini trees. The white oleander died in a hard freeze, the liriope got trashed, and the Bradford pear split in half in a storm. In back, one of the pink crape myrtles died in the plant apocalypse flood of 2016, and my crew moved the other one so it had more room to grow. I gave away the white crape myrtles that didn't bloom to a guy on Craigslist who came and dug them up and took them away. The two mulberry trees and one of the hackberries all rotted and had to come down, and the trumpet vine, as you know, fell when the west fence came down in a storm. Besides those original plantings, I have also lost a lot of things I had added to the garden. Famously, I lost all fifty-plus Knockout roses. I've lost eight dogwoods (I've given up on them in my garden), and a large, beautiful lacebark elm that was just beginning to drape as they so gracefully do, which drowned in the thousand-year flood of 2015. I've lost six or eight different gardenias of various types, trying to find one that can be happy in Dallas, and goodness knows how many camellias have met their maker in my garden, because I can dish out horticultural advice, but apparently I can't take it. I've also lost my three gorgeous six-foot-tall Texas silver sage bushes I adored, a dozen hydrangeas of various kinds and colors, countless irises, and other perennials for reasons ranging from flooding springs and sudden, harsh winter freezes to four years of drought that preceded the floods of 2015 and 2016. Right now, my gigantic rosemary that grew to be fifteen feet across and overhangs the pool is dying a little more each year, and the other hackberry is full of mistletoe, a sure sign it's on its way out.

Yet every spring, no matter the devastation of the preceding year, tiny green points of hope push their way through the ground as life reasserts itself, damaged but undaunted. Over these years, as my garden has received and released so many elements of beauty, it has guided me gently, and sometimes not so gently, in the direction of learning to let go. Every year, my garden accepts far more than it releases, and I have learned that each release brings with it an opportunity for me to create something new and perhaps even better to replace what was lost.

We can't see ourselves grow. We can only feel how differently we respond to events as they happen. Self-awareness is like being in a constant state of peripheral vision. Every time we try to look at ourselves head-on, the focus shifts and we are forced to simply trust the process. Sometimes our friends have a better vantage point to see our growth and how we've changed. When my friend Sophia was here the other night, I told her about an upsetting event that had happened the night before. When I finished, she said, "I'm sorry that happened, but, honey, *look at you*. Five years ago, this would have completely derailed you, and it hasn't. Not at all. You know exactly what you're doing and where you're going. This might have hurt your feelings and made you mad, but it didn't *affect* you. Not really. Not like it used to."

She was right, and I hadn't even noticed it. Five years ago, and for all the years before that, the slightest word of discouragement would have found a fear and doubt receptor inside me, grabbed hold of it, and stopped me in my tracks. I had spent a lifetime at the mercy of everyone else's opinion of how I looked, how I spoke, how I dressed, what I did, my work, my ideas, my opinions, my capacity, my potential...of me. When Sophia said that, I realized just how much I have changed in the last few years. I have accepted responsibility for my life—the good and the bad. I have acknowledged that I have dreams, and I have found the courage to actively work toward making them a reality. I accept that I've made some terrible decisions and colossal mistakes. I've mistreated myself and others. I've allowed myself to be mistreated. And I have forgiven them, and myself. I finally know who I am.

As I look out my window, I realize what I am looking at is not just my garden, it's my life. We have both suffered great losses. We both have periods of immense beauty and richness. We both have times of desolation and emptiness that echo with loneliness. We are both ripe with endless potential. We receive and we let go. We are each always, and forever, a work in progress.

Each morning when we wake, we are a blank canvas waiting to be created anew. Every day is a sacred opportunity to make our lives a work of art. A living, breathing, unique, rarefied, perfectly imperfect work of art with ingredients that only exist within us. And each component that falls away, whether it is a person, a plant, or a possession, was here for a reason and, equally, departs for a reason. Sometimes we hate that and it can take years to recover. Sometimes it brings us great joy, satisfaction, or relief. But either way, each day when we rise, we are called to a new beginning. We have a chance to do or be something more. It is our decision how, or whether, to take advantage of it.

I still haven't done a design for my whole garden, so that opportunity awaits. But I did finally build that wall around the courtyard I wanted when I first bought the house. I drew a full design plan, just like a real landscape designer. Because it was my own house, I made all kinds of design changes on-site while it was being built, but that's part of the fun of working on my own property. And it is beautiful! I love it so much! It was totally worth waiting fourteen years for.

As Fernando and the crew were leaving my house the other evening, after several days of working full-time in my garden, he said, "Okay, is that it? Are we finished?"

I chuckled and said, "You know we're never finished in my garden."

"I know." He beamed, looking around with great pride. "That's why it looks so good."

Epilogue

Into the Great Unknown

It was a quiet, misty day. Soft, gray, and damp. The kind of day I learned to love as a child growing up in Scotland and England. Some people find days like this depressing, but I find that on dark, gray days, introspection comes easily. There is something about the hush of a dark day that stills my mind and opens my heart.

On this morning, I was perusing my garden, slowly letting my eyes pass over each plant with the loving curiosity of a mother noticing small changes happening in her child's face. From my peripheral vision, I noticed a faint hint of motion, and turned for a better view. Before my eyes, dozens of tiny specs were floating past me, hooked lightly on the breeze. At first, I wasn't sure what I was looking at, so I turned to seek a source. There, on a low-hanging crape myrtle branch, was a tiny egg casing, broken open. From it this stream of teensy creatures was emerging, drifting upward like minute bubbles, into the air and away. What were they? What was carrying them? I bent low because they were very, very small, and saw, to my amazement, that they were spiders. Dozens of tiny, newborn spiders meeting the world for the first time.

As I watched them pouring out of their casing, I thought, "What masterful bravery." Unimaginably tiny creatures in a completely unknown place. They have no idea what the world holds. No idea where to go and no navigation to get there. They have no idea what they will find. No idea if it will be safe or not. Yet something that was literally not there before formed inside their minuscule, newly hatched bodies. A filament so fragile it was almost invisible, but they threw it forth into the great unknown, allowing themselves to be caught by the prevailing winds and carried to their destiny. No fear. Only trust.

Thinking about my own life, I'm acutely aware of how much it has been limited by fear. Not in all areas, but in quite a few. How many times I have not done things I wanted to do because I didn't know if I could. I didn't know *how* I could. I didn't know how it would turn out or if I could succeed, so I didn't try. It wasn't that I didn't believe I could succeed, it was simply that I was afraid I *might not* be able to. No reason, only worry and doubt.

There is a powerful line from Shakespeare's *Measure for Measure*: "Our doubts are traitors and make us lose the good we oft might win by fearing to attempt."

And on this day, I got it. It really hit home that every fear I had was a product of my own imagination. I truly got it that self-limitation is antithetical to the very essence of nature's design. We are here to be our fullest expression of creation, and I know that within me there is an innate guidance system that I can trust. Just like those tiny spiders who throw out a filament and wait for the next breeze, trusting it to take them where they need to go, we have the means to allow ourselves to be lifted into the world, carried on the breeze of destiny up to our highest expression. These miraculous bodies of ours have no less genius than those tiny spiders have. There is boldness inside us just waiting to emerge...waiting for us to throw out our filament and see where it takes us. We are equipped with everything we need to go fearlessly forth and seek our destiny in the great unknown. All we need is a little trust.

Let's do it! Grab the filament attached to your dream! I'll race you to the next breeze!

Acknowledgments

In my art and in most other creative areas of my life, I have always been something of an auteur. A solitary, "if you want it done right, do it yourself" kind of girl. But I have learned that isn't scalable. It also isn't true. I've learned that when I am given the opportunity to collaborate with other talented people, something much more amazing emerges than I ever could have created on my own. Writing this book has been one of those opportunities. It truly takes a village. I am blessed to be a part of a particularly brilliant, talented, fun, soulful village, who helped in countless ways to make this dream a reality.

My dearest friend, Helen Seslowsky, for believing in me and my writing so much in its early stages that you convinced me not to self-publish, insisting this book had the potential for a wider audience. Without you, my writing might never have made it outside my circle of friends. I am deeply and eternally grateful for your clear, grounded certainty in the possibility of my dream, even before I had the courage to claim it, and for all of your professional wisdom, insight, input, and assistance. Thank you from the bottom of my heart.

Mary Burch, for so generously sharing your experience as a television producer, your genius for structure, your gift for discerning the most essential elements of story, and especially for the moment you distilled my life into a perfect three-point arc. Your input and notes were absolutely invaluable. Without you, this book would not be what it is. I am in awe of you and I'm eternally grateful.

Dr. Barbara Graham, whose deep, caring counseling, brilliant mind, profound intuition, and great wisdom was transformative in my life. You were the most remarkable mix of tenderness, dynamism, and goddess power I have ever experienced. Thank you for guiding me to a higher purpose and a deeper understanding of self. I miss you terribly, but I know you are now pure Light.

Dr. James Hollis, whose great intellect, eloquent writing, and clear, accessible teachings on the work of Carl Jung were life changing for me. One August afternoon you intellectually knocked me out of the feedback loop of stories from my past with a direct, perspective-shattering personal challenge. Thank you for facilitating such a profound shift in my worldview, and for posing the perfect question to me at the perfect time. The physical reality of this book is a direct result of that day in Rhinebeck.

Acknowledgments

Dr. Gene Helmick-Richardson, entomologist, for your generous help with my questions about spiders and snakes.

Rev. Chris Terry, who was never fooled by any outward circumstances in my life, and could always see my perfect wholeness even (and especially) when I could not. Thank you for holding the high watch for me all those years until I had the courage to emerge from my chrysalis.

Rev. Ellen Debenport, thank you for seeing so much more in me than I saw in myself, particularly as a creator, and for not letting me convince you otherwise.

Rev. Dr. Michael Gott; Rev. Dr. Petra Weldes; Rev. David McClure; Rev. Veronica Valles; Tracy Brown, RScP; Alva Baltimore, RScP; Jan Pearman, LUT; Candace Stowers, RScP; and Rodney Stowers, RScP; plus Chris and Ellen, for being a part of the spiritual/prayer "Team Rebecca."

Unity Church of Dallas; the Center for Spiritual Living, Dallas; and the Dallas Meditation Center. In these safe spaces, I arrived broken, but broken open. Thank you for helping me find my voice, and teaching me that I had within me the tools to transform my life.

The gifted counselors, therapists, body workers, movement facilitators, and healers who have helped me free myself from the traumas of my past, including Dr. Carol Cole; Chris Jones, LPC; Dr. Tyler Lewis; Dr. Amy Gunderson-Lewis; Dr. Leah Garcia; Meggan Perkins; Laurie Cobbley LMT; Jennifer Walz, L.Ac.; Karen Floyd RMT, Reiki Master; Dr. Sherri Fitzgerald; Jen Bagesse LMT; Ronelle Wood MS, SLP, LMT; Dr. Carol Crampton; Anne Olivier LMT, APP; Move Studio; Sunstone Yoga; Toni Bergins, and others.

Acknowledgments

The writings and teachings of Carl Jung, James Hollis, Melody Beattie, Robin Norwood, Venice Bloodworth, Dan Millman, Charles Fillmore, Ernest Holmes, Eric Butterworth, Norman Vincent Peale, Harville Hendrix, Cheryl Richardson, Robert A. Johnson, Joseph Campbell, Joe Dispenza, and many, many others.

Places of refuge and quiet sanctuary, including Orchard Canyon on Oak Creek, Sedona, Arizona; Taos, New Mexico; Ojai, California; Santa Barbara, California; Ventura, California; Wimberely, Texas; and the blue highways of New Zealand.

Heather Jackson, my amazing, brilliant, kind, fierce, heart-centered literary agent, who is both wise and savvy. Thank you for taking a chance on an unknown writer. Thank you for believing in me and my writing. Thank you for your seemingly inexhaustible patience. Thank you for giving me deadlines when I needed them and a free rein when I didn't. You truly "got" me from the beginning, and I am so grateful.

Karen Kosztolnyik, my wonderful editor at Grand Central/Hachette, and sister Texan. I will treasure forever the email you sent me after you finished reading my first draft. Your enthusiastic and encouraging notes throughout this process have meant the world to me. It has been a complete honor and pleasure working with you.

Rachael Kelly, editorial assistant extraordinaire. Thank you so much for being the calm in my storms, and an ever-bright, supportive, cheerful resource for my many (*many . . .*) questions.

Acknowledgments

Karen Murgolo, who acquired this book for Grand Central Life & Style/Hachette. Your love of this project changed not only the course of my life, but how I view myself. Thank you.

Jannette Anderson, Brad Hart, and Charlie Hoehn, the trifecta of generous super-connectors constituting the penultimate leg of my Rube Goldberg path to being published.

The people who have encouraged, supported, and helped me in myriad ways, both personally and professionally, before, during, and after the development of this book, including Susan Shankin, Donna Collins, Monica Hochberg, Susan Keller, and especially Olga Diaz.

My sister, Betsy Main, and the friends who held my hand and heart during the life upheavals which ultimately became the resources for this book. My gratitude for your love and friendship is without measure.

My mother, Betty Muir Ogden Oberthier Brantly. I so wish you could be here to share this with me. I love you and miss you so much.

My son, Alexander Winn, my alpha and my omega. My most steadfast and forever cheerleader, editor, inspiration, rock, sounding board, brainstorming partner, and my greatest achievement. I love you more than the whole world covered in diamonds.

About the Author

Rebecca Winn is a multiple award-winning landscape designer and creator of the inspirational Facebook blog *Whimsical Gardens*. Her eye for nature's beauty and her unique blend of wisdom, insight, and humor inspire and entertain hundreds of thousands of readers around the globe each day. Born in Dallas, Texas, Rebecca's family moved to Europe when she was in first grade, providing her the opportunity to grow up surrounded by the majestic, centuries-old gardens of Italy, Scotland, and England, which strongly influenced both her garden designs and her writing. Her articles have appeared in regional and national magazines. *One Hundred Daffodils* is her first book.